Second Thoughts on the Family

Anastasia de Waal

Civitas: Institute for the Study of Civil Society
London
Registered Charity No. 1085494

First Published May 2008

© Civitas 2008
77 Great Peter Street
London SW1P 2EZ
Civitas is a registered charity (no. 1085494)
and a company limited by guarantee, registered in
England and Wales (no. 04023541)

email: books@civitas.org.uk

All rights reserved

ISBN 978-1-903386-65-1

Independence: Civitas: Institute for the Study of Civil Society is a registered educational charity (No. 1085494) and a company limited by guarantee (No. 04023541). Civitas is financed from a variety of private sources to avoid over-reliance on any single or small group of donors.

All publications are independently refereed. All the Institute's publications seek to further its objective of promoting the advancement of learning. The views expressed are those of the authors, not of the Institute.

Typeset by
Civitas

Printed in Great Britain by
The Cromwell Press
Trowbridge, Wiltshire

Contents

page

Author	v
Acknowledgements and Author's Note	v
Executive Summary	vi
Introduction	1

The Interviews

Anthony Giddens	15
Charles Murray	19
Michael Lamb	22
Terri Apter	26
Susie Orbach	29
Linda Papadopoulos	31
Jenni Murray	34
Jenny Watson	38
Polly Toynbee	43
Linda Bellos	50
Fay Weldon	55
Jo Elvin	61
Marie O'Riordan	63
Deborah Joseph	67
Deidre Sanders	71
Virginia Ironside	76
Libby Brooks	79
Kate Bell	81
Peter Tatchell	84
Duncan Fisher	87
Sue Burridge	93
Esther Rantzen	98
Kate Green	104
Cherie Booth	106
Tim Loughton	111
Annette Brooke	115
Harriet Harman	120

	page
Interview Analysis	125
The Survey: Gauging Attitudes to Marriage Amongst Young People in Britain	145
The Survey: Findings in Full	154
Conclusion	178
Policy Recommendations	190
Appendix 1	193
Appendix 2	222
Notes	226

Author

Anastasia de Waal is Head of Family and Education at Civitas. Holding a BSc and MSc in Sociology from the London School of Economics, she is also a qualified primary school teacher, trained specifically for teaching in the inner city. Anastasia is author of *Inspection, Inspection, Inspection* (2006) and several reports on the state education system. She is a regular contributor to print and broadcast media, panellist for the *Observer* and board member of Women's Parliamentary Radio.

Acknowledgements and Author's Note

This project has required much help and patience from all those involved. Thanks are due to each distinguished interviewee who kindly agreed to take part, and special thanks due to Kathleen Kiernan, Boni Sones, Anthony Giddens and Claire Daley for whose comments I am very grateful.

It is important to note that the views expressed in sections of the book other than the interviews are not necessarily supported by interviewees.

Executive Summary

Politics and the family

As one of the last remaining areas of division between the two main political parties, the family is a central battleground of British politics. On the one hand, the Conservative Party believes that the two-parent family needs to be promoted by providing financial incentives to marry. On the other, the Labour Party has taken up a 'neutral' position on the family in which structure doesn't matter. Both positions are out of touch with reality:

- Marriage does not need to be 'incentivised': despite declining marriage rates and a high number of divorces, marriage is arguably more popular today than ever before. It is no longer 'necessary' to marry socially, yet it is the most common form of partnership with or without children[1] in Britain today and new research commissioned for *Second Thoughts on the Family* shows that 70 per cent of a representative sample of British young people would like to get married.

- Family structure in the UK *should* matter to Labour because of a hugely significant trend underlying it. The 'diverse' family today is disproportionately likely to be the 'poor' family. The obstacles economic strains present to stability mean that lower income families are considerably more likely to be unmarried and separated.[2]

The real issue

Distracted by political positioning, each party has exaggerated the degree of choice in UK family life. The premise of both New Labour and Conservative policy is that those people not living in married two-parent families are simply *choosing* not to. This is interpreted as a sign of positive diversity by Labour and a decline in family values by the Conservatives. Both sides miss a critical reality which should be of central concern to family policy: namely the correlation between low-income and family instability.

This relationship between poverty and family structure, together with the high marital rates on the Left in the middle and upper classes, lead to the conclusion that the true divide over the family today is a *class* rather than a political one—and that marriage has become a luxury good.

EXECUTIVE SUMMARY

A snapshot of the true family divide in the UK

The Millennium Cohort Study, a nationally representative survey of the families of children born around the year 2000, reveals the stark relationship between parenting partnerships and socio-economic status in Britain today:[3]

- At the time of birth, 68 per cent of married parents, 56 per cent of cohabiting parents and 35 per cent of single parents lived in the *advantaged* areas sampled.

- By contrast, 26 per cent of married parents, 43 per cent of cohabiting parents and 55 per cent of single parents lived in the *disadvantaged* areas sampled.

The difference between parenting partnerships and educational level in the Millennium Cohort Study is equally acute:

- Amongst those who were single parents at the time of their child's birth, 28 per cent had no qualifications, amongst those cohabiting 13 per cent had no qualifications and amongst those who were married just eight per cent had no qualifications.

- By contrast, 43 per cent of mothers who were married at the time of their child's birth had the highest level of qualifications, amongst those cohabiting the proportion was 24 per cent, and amongst single parents just ten per cent had the highest level of qualifications.

Why family structure and marriage should matter to both Left and Right

Structural poverty
Lower marital rates in low-income areas, greater numbers of cohabiting parents, higher divorce rates and more single-parent families amongst the less well-off are strongly connected to 'structural poverty': that is, unemployment-related family instability leading to further poverty due to parental separation. Low-income through un/under-employment causes parental separation—and parental separation causes lower-income. For New Labour, this relationship between family structure and economics is vital because it is a central contributor to child poverty.

Marriage
Marriage has shifted from being a moral Conservative Party issue to a pragmatic issue relating to personal aspirations—and crucially, social

exclusion. Whilst 70 per cent of children born within marriage will live their entire childhood (to their sixteenth birthday) with both natural parents, this is the case for only 36 per cent of children born into a cohabiting union. Significantly, a disproportionate number of cohabiting parents come from disadvantaged areas.[4]

In the UK, marriage's longevity compared to cohabitation is explained by the key differentiating factor: commitment. Getting married today is both an indicator of couples' mutual commitment and circumstances conducive to it: i.e. marriage signals (rather than generates) commitment. This association with commitment helps to explain why people are continuing to marry when they can simply cohabit and why cohabitation is generally considered to be a precursor to rather than substitute for marriage. It is noteworthy that the highest proportion of respondents wanting to marry in the Civitas Ipsos MORI survey are cohabitants.

Addressing parental separation is vital to tackling child poverty

Child poverty is currently concentrated in single-parent families. Whilst New Labour has sought to mitigate single-parent household poverty, it is not paying attention to the circumstances leading to single parenthood. At present the Labour government concentrates on dealing with the outcomes of parental separation. A more ambitious strategy would be to focus on addressing the causes of parental separation *as well as* dealing with the outcomes. The aim should be to look at the bigger picture and the longer-term, adding a complementary *pro*active dimension to their current *re*active approach.

Stabilising families

Ultimately, the aim of family policy should be to foster stability. Stability is achieved through well-functioning arrangements regarding work, childcare and the interface, continuity for children, and the fulfilment of parental responsibilities by both mothers and fathers. Instability in family life denotes and leads to difficulties for children and parents. Working to achieve stability does not mean forcing dysfunctional families to stay together; on the contrary it means fostering parenting partnerships which work and ensuring continuity in the event of parental separation.

EXECUTIVE SUMMARY

Family structure: important in both intact families and separated ones

Fostering stable relationships is key, but equally important is securing the continuation of the family unit *after* separation. The significance of 'structure' therefore, refers to more than intact parenting partnerships. In terms of the responsibility of co-parenting, structure is relevant right across family types: from same-sex adopted families to single-parent families, as in the majority of cases parenting started out as a partnership. Structure ought to refer as much to the parenting model as to the relationship between parents. For this reason it would be useful to stop talking about family breakdown and start talking about parental separation. The parents may split, but the family unit—the parenting structure—should remain intact. One of the main reasons that the children of separated parents are more likely to face difficulties is because the two-parent structure in terms of responsibility—the 'dual-parenting'—collapses.

Policy Recommendations

Youth employment and education

Weaknesses in the education system coupled with potential welfare dependency have generated a high level of educational and economic inactivity amongst young people in the UK. The number of young people 'not in education, employment or training'—NEETs—has risen by 15 per cent under New Labour.[5] Patterns in family formation show a strong relationship between unemployment and the young, poor and unstable family. The way to impact on this problematic scenario is both through educational provision which has more relevance to pupils' futures, particularly in relation to vocational education, and through the restructuring of the terms of unemployment entitlements in order to lessen the likelihood of stagnant welfare reliance.

Tax arrangements

Income-splitting

Informal childcare should be recognised within income tax arrangements for registered parents (regardless of marital status). This would be possible through a tax system which accounted for the dependent status of children as well as non-working and low-earning (for example through part-time employment) partners by pooling the family income, dividing it by a quotient based on family size, and applying the relevant tax formula according to income level. This would help increase recognition of childcare as well as facilitate it and help foster mutual (rather than one-way) dependency and an equal division of labour between parents.

Non-resident parent responsibility

Financial child support

Child maintenance needs to be simplified and universalised by being taken automatically out of wages or social assistance (whatever the income earned or unearned) through HM Revenue and Customs. Parents should not be left to come to an informal arrangement. In the event of separation, non-resident working parents should also continue to receive a dependent tax-break (as outlined above) on their income as long as they are eligible for child maintenance.

Mediation within divorce proceedings

Mediation between divorcing parents should be a central element and statutory requirement of the divorce process. The purpose of mediation would be primarily to work through the practical and financial arrangements between parents regarding childcare post-separation but also to open potential channels for reconciliation.

Childcare

Transferable parental leave

Maternity leave taken post-pregnancy should be made transferable to the father. This would enable greater parenting equality between mothers and fathers, expand parents' options and lessen potential employer discrimination of women on the basis that they 'might get pregnant'. Furthermore this would help mitigate what is perceived to be a 'gender' pay gap but is in practice chiefly a *parenting* pay gap.

Introduction

Over the last 100 years family life in the UK has seen many changes. Cohabitation has become very common as has having children outside marriage. Divorce and parental separation have also become everyday phenomena resulting in a concurrent rise in stepfamilies and single parenting. Driving these changes have been structural shifts accompanied by cultural and legislative ones.

A major structural change has been women's mass entrance into the labour force as well as higher rates of entry into further and higher education. One of the most significant consequences of women participating in paid labour has been the attainment of potential economic independence from a male breadwinner. This has had major repercussions for relations between men and women, and in turn family life. Women have ceased to 'need' to marry in the same way. They can now leave marriage and survive economically. Secondly, family is no longer the only priority for women. This has led to postponed and/or forgone marriage and childbearing. Women today are less likely to have children, they are more likely to have fewer children and they are more likely to spend less time with their children. Female employment has also affected men's relations with children. As women have gone into paid work, men have become involved in childcare on an unprecedented level. A shift in gender relations, largely through women's employment, has furthermore entailed a shift in the meaning of marriage.

Legislative and cultural change has also had a significant impact on family life. Tied to the shifts in women's working lives have been influences on social and sexual mores. Whilst 'First Wave' feminism, active at end of nineteenth and the start of the twentieth century, fought for women's statutory equality and access to higher education, the 'Second Wave' feminism of the 1960s and 1970s homed in on perceived inequality between men and women in domestic life. With the status quo under attack, the norm of the married family with the male breadwinner and homemaker wife was the obvious target. Marriage came most heavily under fire, although some feminists also proposed that women reject the nuclear family and even men. While mainstream society did not adopt such a radical stance, the impact of feminist thinking was the problematisation of the married family.

Legislative changes are one consequence of feminist influence and the pursuit for greater parity between men and women. Contraception, for example, has been made universally available to all and divorce laws have been relaxed. The availability of contraception has allowed sex to be separated from parenting; the availability of divorce means that marriage need no longer be a lifetime commitment.

Whilst the seeds of transformation were sown through the 1960s and 1970s, the structure of the family picture in the UK shifted most acutely during the 1980s and 1990s to the one we see today. Economic restructuring led to widespread unemployment leaving many families in economic uncertainty. One effect of economic strains was a rise in parental separation. The concurrent decline in marriage rates, some sociologists argue, essentially came about as unemployed men became less desirable husband material.

What is significant about the growth of the diverse—generally fragmented—family in the UK is that it was intellectually normalised by the upper classes but then practised *en masse* by the working (or often work*less*) classes. By the 1980s and 1990s, many of those who had sympathised with the feminist perspectives of the 1960s and 1970s found that marriage and family were now compatible with the pursuit of gender equality. Marriage, as historian Stephanie Coontz argues, became a choice,[1] and if anything those with more choices, i.e. the more affluent, were disproportionately choosing it. Similarly, although divorce is widespread today, as are cohabitation and single parenting, there are strong relationships between all three and background disadvantage. In Coontz's words: 'For centuries, women with independent means and minds were less likely to marry, and if they did marry, more likely to divorce, than women with lower levels of education and earnings.' Today however the situation has reversed: 'In both the United States and Britain, women with college degrees or good jobs are now more likely to marry and less likely to divorce than women with lower education and earnings.'[2]

Since the end of the 1980s in particular, there has been a shift in the meaning of marriage and, connected to that, the desirability of the two-parent family. Marriage has become increasingly detached from its past connotations and treated not as a vacuum in which either gender inequality or equality breed, but rather as a reflector of relations between men and women in wider society. With marriage today seen to be a personal commitment to a partner as much as it was perceived to be an institution designed around a gendered division of labour in the past, there has been a realisation that throwing marriage out with inequality between men and women is unnecessary.

In its 'Third Wave', marriage and the two-parent family are generally acceptable to feminism; marrying is no longer seen as selling out to patriarchy. In this country today marriage does not simply constitute a nostalgic throwback. The commitment it appears to signify to couples is highly significant to parenting. Many self-declared feminists are married, as are their children. The commitment which marriage represents is increasingly acknowledged as a positive: for adults, in that it facilitates shared parenting, for children, in that it facilitates stability. Nevertheless *supporting* marriage, as opposed to privately aspiring and subscribing to it, is still seen to be out-dated. There continue to be significant hang-ups within the New Labour government to talking openly about the family, leading to a disconnection between Labour politicians' personal beliefs and their political rhetoric. Discussion of disadvantageous circumstances and ways of fostering parenting stability are marred by a tangible political correctness. There is a fear that even talking positively about, as opposed to privileging, marriage and two-parent families, implies negativity towards other family arrangements such as separated or same-sex families. Policy-wise, most explicitly since the 1983 Labour Party Manifesto, Labour has sought to support a 'wide variety' of families, launching a critical campaign against the Conservatives for not doing so.[3] New Labour's attempted neutrality has resulted in the symbolic removal of the Married Couples Allowance and an avoidance of rhetorical and fiscal support for couple-families. Its preferred stance is to deal practically with the outcomes of parental separation such as poverty, supporting children rather than particular family structures.

The Right, on the other hand, not having had the same relationship with either feminism or democratic diversity, has been more inclined to maintain the status quo over the last hundred years. Throughout the twentieth century the Conservative Party strove to bolster the family unit with marriage at the centre, ostensibly with the aim of asserting interdependence in the family to displace dependence on the state. This support has tended to be rhetorical rather than legislative. Today under David Cameron, the Conservatives have continued to champion marriage and the two-parent family unit. The emphasis has shifted a little to focus more explicitly on child welfare under the auspices of 'compassionate' Conservatism, with the beneficial outcomes of stability for children the main purported rationale for supporting the married family. This 'updating' of the Conservative stance on marriage has done little to mitigate their moralising reputation, merely displacing notions of social irresponsibility with parental irresponsibility.

This report

On the ground, this Labour/Conservative, Left/Right divide on the family looks outdated; as do both parties' interpretations of what people want. The common aspiration for committed relationships, especially when it comes to parenting, regardless of politics and sexuality and against a backdrop of new-found choice, suggests that society shares more in common than divides it. Party politics is failing to see that greater acceptance of diversity is compatible with fostering committed family relationships—and vice versa. The aim of this report is to explore whether there is perhaps a new consensus on what our priorities for adult relationships and the family are and therefore whether the family can be shifted from being treated as a political football to a common goal.

The interviews

The report has been called *Second Thoughts on the Family* because it questions the existing political divide, opinion formers and young people in order to identify what government should be striving for in family policy. In order to explore policy priorities for the family, two pieces of research have been carried out. The first is a series of interviews with opinion formers, picked predominantly from what can be broadly defined as either left-wing or 'neutral' standpoints. The rationale behind this deliberate imbalance is to look beyond the views traditionally associated with the political right for three particular reasons.

Firstly, those linked with conservatism have to-date tended to be both more explicit and more vociferous about their priorities for the family: notably, attaching a high value to the 'traditional' family. The liberalism of those more closely associated with the Left, by contrast, has tended to entail a neutral public position, which carefully attaches no preference to particular family forms. The aim therefore has been to analyse how much of this neutrality reflects an ambivalence towards family structures and how much relates to aspirations of broad-mindedness and inclusiveness. The second motivation for focusing on the Left is quite straightforwardly to concentrate on those views which are more likely to influence current government policy. The third rationale is perhaps the most significant: to demonstrate the way in which the Labour Party's reluctance to problematise family instability on the grounds that 'families come in all shapes and sizes' has blurred the lines between the diverse and the deprived family—a nominally politically correct position which in reality disregards the difficulties of precisely those it strives to protect.

In twenty-first century Britain the most common alternatives to the 'traditional' (married, two-parent) family are the unmarried and separated family—and both are found disproportionately amongst those on lower incomes. What are construed as positive manifestations of diversity and freedom are in fact very often *negative* manifestations of deprivation and limiting circumstances. This is not to deny that new opportunities to end unhappy relationships and a greater freedom of choice in family life have positively affected families right across the socio-economic spectrum. However, non-marriage and parental separation in the UK today disproportionately represent the problematic, as opposed to the progressive, elements of family diversity.

Neither Labour nor the Conservatives satisfactorily acknowledge the role of economics in family structure. Both parties have exaggerated agency in their interpretation of family life. The assumption is that people are not living in married two-parent families because they are choosing not to; new 'choices' regarded as positive by New Labour and problematic by the Conservative Party. This highly middle-class-centric view fails to acknowledge *thwarted* opportunity amongst the lower socio-economic classes.

As historian Stephanie Coontz argues, breaking with the past, today we appear to have moved on to a phase of family patterns where stability in partnership and parenting has become the domain of the better off. This reality transforms marriage (fundamentally significant here because it is the most statistically stable form of union we have in this country) and the two-parent family from traditionally conservative preoccupations into ones highly relevant to left-wing priorities. Whilst the Right's conceptualisation of parental separation does not fit with left-wing concerns, it is misguided for the Left to simply disregard family structure. An interest in family stability does not constitute a conservative approach to the family: the New Labour government needs to examine parental separation on their own terms, for the purposes of their own democratising agenda.

New Labour has placed more emphasis on increasing life chances and tackling social exclusion than any other government to date. Eradicating child poverty lies at the heart of their agenda—and rightly so. The emphasis on tackling child poverty is imperative because of the limitations that living in poor households place on children's life chances. On virtually every indicator low-income negatively affects a child's outcomes. Short-term strategies are vital to alleviating child poverty on an immediate basis. However policy also needs to address the factors contributing to the home context: the child's family circumstances. Significantly, child poverty is currently concentrated in single-parent families. Whilst New Labour has sought to mitigate single-parent household poverty it is not paying attention to the circumstances generating entry into single parenthood. The less well-off are disproportionately likely to separate because economic constraints generate obstacles to domestic stability. Poverty is particularly pertinent to parental separation as, when parents do separate, children very often experience a drop in household income. Therefore poverty both contributes to parental separation and parental separation to poverty.

The families of children in the Millennium Cohort Study, a large-scale longitudinal research programme tracking the outcomes of children born in the UK around the year 2000, illustrate the strength of this relationship:

> There was a very strong link between partnership status and poverty. Married parents were least likely to be in the poverty income bracket (14.5 per cent), followed by cohabiting respondents (30.4 per cent). Lone parents were the most likely to be below the threshold on their own income (72.1 per cent).[4]

Politically, a fresh focus on the family is entirely plausible for the Left. The relationship today between family structure and economics means that it would not represent a U-turn for the Left to start scrutinising patterns of parental separation. Quite the reverse, doing so would represent a responsiveness to the British family context in keeping with the Left's pursuit thus far of a more democratic family. It is rather Labour's failure to acknowledge the link between family fragility and poverty which is anathema to the left-wing agenda of tackling social exclusion. Furthermore, the 'solutions'—the routes to family stability—are structural, relating in particular to employment and education amongst young people, rather than to moralising or dictation on the basis of what is considered 'best'.

To reiterate, to critique the Left and Labour Party policy in the report is not to advocate Conservative Party policy. On the contrary, New Labour's current position on the family relates strongly to those Conservative policies which have been misguidedly moralistic and ineffective. As outlined, the purpose of focusing on the Left is rather to illustrate the way in which an updated approach to the family is essential to addressing social exclusion and to fostering social equality.

Returning to the selection of interviewees in the report, three thinkers have been chosen to represent political, academic and religious thinking which is associated with support for the two-parent, married family. These are Tim Loughton, the Conservative spokesperson for Children, Young People and Families, the sociologist Charles Murray, and Sue Burridge, family policy adviser to the Church of England.

Amongst the remaining 24 interviewees are contributors to public opinion through research (academic specialists), through policy (politicians), through campaigning (charities and lobbying groups) and through media commentary (writers and commentators). These interviewees have been chosen to include views representing feminist and left-wing thinking, party-political beliefs, scholarly research and the perceived aspirations and concerns of young people.

There are two noticeable characteristics in the make-up of the overall interviewee selection. Firstly, a disproportionate number of women have been interviewed (only six out of a total of 27 are male); there is also a very strong middle-class voice. These points which might be perceived as weaknesses, arguably convey the way in which thinking on the family—particularly on the Left—is currently being shaped.

Marriage survey
The second strand of the research homes in on an issue central to current political debate over family: marriage. Marriage connects most strongly with the family of the past and has caused the most contention between the political parties. In addition, changes to marriage and

marital patterns have had a transformative influence on the modern family, whilst at the same time the majority of families with dependent children are headed by married parents. Furthermore, marital patterns are, as mentioned, heavily influenced by socio-economic background. To understand the future of marriage by gauging its meaning today, a survey of 1,560 young people's attitudes to marrying has been carried out using Ipsos MORI. The aim has been to understand whether getting married is an aspiration amongst 20-35 year-olds in Britain; if so, why? And if not, why not?

Extensive research of both the influential and those on the ground has led to a fascinating insight into the family 'problem' today: an awkward schism between shared goals and ideological divides which explains why it is that we can think along similar lines, across politics, when it comes to what we want for our own families. The relationship between poverty and family structure, together with the high marital rates on the Left in the middle and upper classes, lead to the conclusion that the true divide over the family today is a *class* rather than a political one—and that marriage has become a luxury good.

The interviews

Whose interviews appear in the report?

The write-ups of 27 interviews have been included, ranging from social theorist Anthony Giddens to author and 'former' feminist author Fay Weldon. The interviewees provide a range of perspectives on issues relating to family life, as well as a range of different angles. Some, for example, focus on children, others on adults and some on their particular 'concern group', single parents for example. Two supplementary interviews with sociologists Catherine Hakim and Rosemary Crompton inform a central preoccupation for many of the interviewees, juggling employment and childcare.

How have the interviewees been selected?

The interviewees have been chosen on the basis of their having a connection with family life, although not necessarily an immediately obvious one. The aim has been to look further than the 'usual suspects' (as well as to include some) at the question of 'what priorities should be for the family'. It is important to emphasise right from the start that the interviewees were not chosen according to any 'scientific' criteria, but rather at the author's discretion.

Amongst the academic selection, sociologists Anthony Giddens and Charles Murray provide insights into what lies behind social change in relation to the family. Developmental and social psychologists Michael Lamb and Terri Apter discuss the impact of diverse forms of family life on children and adults, as well as the best way to address new dilemmas. Psychoanalyst Susie Orbach and chartered psychologist Linda Papadopoulos throw some light on the ways in which relationships between men and women, and mothers and fathers, have changed.

With the debate on the family closely connected to issues around gender relations, the views of those associated with past and present forms of feminism are of particular interest. The interviewees in this group span from *Woman's Hour* presenter Jenni Murray, a vociferous feminist over the years and current President of the gender equality lobbying organisation the Fawcett Society, to the then-Chair of the Equal Opportunities Commission, Jenny Watson, the *Guardian's* Polly Toynbee, activist Linda Bellos, the first black woman to join the feminist group *Spare Rib,* and 'post-feminist' novelist Fay Weldon.

Connected to the group above is a sub-section of interviewees selected on the grounds of being in touch with young women today. These include Jo Elvin, editor of Britain's best-selling women's magazine *Glamour,* Marie O'Riordan, editor of the magazine regarded as the intelligent magazine for 'empowered' women, *Marie Claire,* and Deborah Joseph, editor of *Brides Magazine,* the UK's best-selling weddings magazine. From the editors of *Glamour* and *Marie Claire,* the interest was in gauging young women's aspirations around the family, and from the editor of *Brides Magazine,* the picture around marriage and weddings today. A rationale behind this focus on young women's aspirations was to compare them with the aspirations of Second Wave feminism. Within this sub-section come two 'agony aunts', Deidre Sanders, problem page editor of the *Sun,* and her counterpart at the *Independent,* Virginia Ironside. Both the *Sun* and the *Independent* have young but contrasting readership profiles in terms of socio-economic class and political conviction. An additional point is that Virginia Ironside and Deidre Sanders come from a generation heavily influenced by 1960s feminism, a subject on which Sanders has written.[5] The aim was to gain some insight into the concerns of their respective readers around the family as well as to listen to Sanders' and Ironside's assessment of family life today and priorities for tomorrow. Libby Brooks, deputy comment editor of the *Guardian* and author of *The Story of Childhood: Growing Up in Modern Britain*,[6] is the final interviewee in this section. As a young feminist, Brooks provides an insight into the interface between what is good for women today in relation to gender equality and what is good for children in relation to parenting arrangements.

The next group consists of interviewees representing some of the family-related issues which have come to the fore. This group ranges from the Head of Policy and Research at One Parent Families/Gingerbread, Kate Bell, to gay rights activist Peter Tatchell, Duncan Fisher, co-founder of the Fatherhood Institute, and the Church of England's family policy adviser, Sue Burridge. The interest in talking to these interviewees was to understand the issues they are seeking to tackle, how they perceive family policy to be doing in relation to their particular concerns, and what they would like to see on the family policy agenda in the future.

Related to this sub-section is the group consisting of those championing the rights and protection of children. These interviewees are Esther Rantzen, founder of ChildLine, Kate Green, Chief Executive of Child Poverty Action Group and Cherie Booth, then President of Barnardo's. The aim was to listen to each of their sets of priorities for happy, healthy children as well as their analyses of children's lives in Britain today.

The final category is made up of Members of Parliament from the three main political parties. To discuss current and future family policy the Conservative and Liberal Democrat spokespersons for Children, Young People and Families were interviewed, with Harriet Harman, Minister for Justice at the time of interview, representing the Labour Party.

Many of the interviewees 'double-up' in the perspectives that they provide; Harriet Harman, for example, is a member of the New Labour government Cabinet, a long-time campaigner for gender equality through legislation, and the force behind the government's National Childcare Strategy. Anthony Giddens's Third Way theories arguably transformed Labour into New Labour.

INTRODUCTION

How were the interviews done?

All but one of the interviews were carried out either over the phone or in person, and in many cases a combination of the two. Cherie Booth submitted written answers to a set of general questions via email. Written notes were taken throughout the interviews rather than an audio recording.

The decision not to record any of the interviews was made when two interviewees at the start of the process expressed a preference not to be taped. In the interest of consistency the decision was made to rely on note-taking for all the interviews.

Interviewees were given the opportunity to alter and/or add to the write-up of their interview. In some ways offering interviewees the chance to change their responses is the last thing a researcher wants; particularly on such a heavily politicised topic, it may well lead to self-censorship. However, as well as the need to clear the interview in light of a lack of an objective record, this 'collaborative' process has had benefits. Firstly, it is likely that a number of the interviewees would not have agreed to be interviewed without being given the opportunity to check the write-up in order to ensure a presentation of their views which they were happy with. Secondly, allowing interviewees to check and alter the write-ups, together with the fact that there would be no indisputable record, arguably led to more spontaneous answers. Thirdly, it was of particular interest to see whether people *did* feel, in retrospect, that they wanted to remove things which they had said at the time; it provided an insight into any disparities between what people think and what they feel they can *say* they think. For example, one interviewee who had argued that (s)he considered a man and a woman to provide the ideal parenting scenario for children, decided on reflection to remove the point. This in itself was an illuminating insight into current sensitivities on the family as well as some of the issues policy-making faces. On the whole, however, only a few interviewees did opt to alter or add to their interview, and generally changes were not substantial. Nevertheless, from the alterations which were made a clear theme emerged; changes tended to be 'tempering' ones where interviewees were concerned about over-generalising or sounding in some way discriminatory. Overall, there was a common concern about appearing to be judgemental.

No single set of questions was asked. Instead a skeleton of topics was put to each interviewee relating to change and continuity in the family, issues and priorities for families and children, and the specific perspective on the family of the interviewee in their professional capacity. In some cases the interviews developed more as conversations, in others more as structured interviews. The variation in style is reflected in their write-ups.

The Interviews

Anthony Giddens
Sociologist and author of *The Third Way*

Professor Anthony Giddens is a sociologist and member of the House of Lords. His theories have contributed significantly to the Labour Party's rebirth as New Labour.

If one thing concerns Anthony Giddens about family in the UK today, it's fertility. 'The low birth rate is a serious structural issue: we need to get parents back to the situation where they want more children. It is possible that immigrants may come to our rescue, since they have more children on average than the indigenous population. Indeed, the birth rate at the moment is climbing again. But we can't count upon migrants in the longer term, since they adapt to indigenous patterns.

'The low birth rate relates to huge structural changes witnessed in society, with the single biggest influence on the family being the partial emancipation of women. In the labour force in particular, there has been an acceptance of greater equality on both sides and this has had wider implications.'

He talks of 'partial' female emancipation, he explains, because he sees gender divides as still prevalent. 'There is a fear of female sexuality. In this respect there isn't sexual equality as men continue to "prey" on women. Added to that, there is far more equality than there was, but women still have to do the "double shift" and are still the primary carers.

'The progress has been more than halfway though, affecting in particular women's careers. There are far more women in the professions, more doctors and in law it's about 50/50. The remaining problem is women not getting to the same level as men. But it will be another 30 years before we know if this will change. It is happening in other countries however: Scandinavia is a good example of successful emancipation.'

Giddens sees Scandinavia's exemplary childcare as key to this emancipation. 'Besides,' he adds, 'a lot of women doing unpaid caring labour generally, will be problematic for pensions.'

Overall shifts in social life have transformed the family, Giddens argues. 'The family is becoming postmodern. It is fundamentally different on several levels, for example with new technologies of reproduction—science has invaded nature. Gay relationships also represent significant change in society. Across the world there is a religious Right which is against gay relationships in the name of preserving the traditional family. And even though it is not so pronounced in this country, it still exists.

'There is a need to modernise family values. They currently disqualify many people in situations which "traditional" values do not accommodate.'

Far from weakening the family, Giddens considers social and economic change to be strengthening it. 'The extended family is becoming more and more important: communications and connections, advances in technology, mobility and technology mean that people are able to keep in touch across the world on a daily basis. The family is still a very powerful thing.'

He sees greater paternal involvement in childcare as another sign of stronger modern families. 'Despite arguments that the family is weakening, it's not weakening. For example fathers are now spending much more time with their kids than they were in the 1950s, when there was the father-as-breadwinner model. The other thing is that children apparently now remain much closer to their parents when they've left home than they did in the past.'

Crucial to our perception of family life today, Giddens argues, is greater realism about the family of the past. 'There is a nostalgia for a "mythical" family. The traditional family was useful because it was a system of obligation and duty. But there were many bad things in the family such as the sexual exploitation of women, and abuse. The dark side was huge. There was never a true "golden age".

'Stephanie Coontz is right: we need to stop being so black and white about the family and how it's changed. The family is far more democratised now, different forms of family structure are perceived more equally.'

Nevertheless Giddens sees that there are social issues around the family as well as social change. 'But there is no magic bullet, which is more or less contrary to what the Conservatives believe. Under New Labour lone parents have got far more chance of doing well now. In these areas there is more than poverty: there is a generic phenomenon of what poverty is, including family difficulties, this is why the standardising term "social exclusion" is now used.'

He also sees socio-economic class as relevant to marriage. 'Poverty makes it very difficult to keep a relationship going. And we know from research that women don't want unskilled men. The other issue is that now there are increasing economic family divides with selective mating—where like people marry like—which is producing more inequality.'

When it comes to parental separation he sees sorting the positives from the negatives as complex. 'It's difficult to say where the balance lies. We want to support commitment as a government, but we need to recognise the realities of life. The principle of children first, the principle which this government has adopted, is a good one but a difficult one to achieve in practice.'

Giddens sees clear divisions between the Left and Right on the family. 'There is a long-standing political divide between a more conservative side which tends to support what they call the "traditional family" although in fact it's not really a traditional family but an idealised version of the 1950s family that never was.

'The Left, on the other hand, has a broader view which accepts that family life has changed and that there is no going back. For example, the fact that single-parent families are like others—a much more post-modern version of the family that accepts that there are a whole range of family types. But we shouldn't penalise other family types. They have conceded on the Left about marriage,' he adds, 'but only to a point.

'But there is also a moderate Left, and I'm part of it, that sees that marriage is a significant thing and that we need to support it and not penalise it.'

Yet despite supporting marriage—'I've got to be an advocate of marriage, I've been married three times'—he disagrees strongly with the Conservatives' presentation of it. 'I've been trawling through Iain Duncan Smith's report this morning and marriage has been elevated above all else. One mustn't fetishise marriage—the important thing is good parenting and the children, and therefore we mustn't penalise those that don't get married. A small tax break is not going to persuade people to get married who wouldn't otherwise.'

Giddens finds it ironic that the Conservatives champion marriage whilst simultaneously attacking state intervention into the family. 'Institutions such as marriage are very much state phenomena. The family is never going to be separated from the state, they are very much intertwined.'

He sees the enforcement of paternal responsibility as definitely a beneficial form of state intervention. 'The government has to be in favour of being draconian. Every parent has a more or less lifetime responsibility to their children and there should be sanctions for those that don't take responsibility. But we must also recognise that men might have two or three families, that on the ground there are also practical issues. The policy of putting children first is a good one—IDS on the other hand, says put marriage first, I think.'

Despite support for opening up the family, Giddens does think that there are 'ideal' families. 'Two parents who get on is better than two parents who don't, and we know that the evidence shows that on the whole children in two-parent families do better. Of course family structure matters—but you can't legislate to pull things back. You can certainly say that there is an ideal of a family where the two parents care for each other and their children, but there's no going back to the traditional family.'

Giddens regards marriage as also having a new trajectory. 'People used to ask whether you were married, as a woman, but now people ask whether you are in a relationship. Politics has been mediated by the mass media and there is now an expectation that people's relationships are judged all the same. In adult relationships we are witnessing the "Sex and the City" phenomenon where people have multiple partners before marriage.'

Similarly: 'Marriage is never going to go back to being a lifetime thing. There is a mutual commitment to sustain in marriage, which in the past was linked to the traditional roles of men and women. Marriage can stabilise but you cannot go against structural trends.'

Giddens's own family life, he argues, is quintessentially of today. 'I have two children from my first marriage, who I have very good relationships with—and a stepdaughter, who I also think I have a very good relationship with. So you could say I'm thoroughly post-modern.'

Charles Murray
Sociologist

Dr Charles Murray is an American public policy analyst and co-author of The Bell Curve: Intelligence and Class Structure in American Life.

Charles Murray sees the modern family as having undergone a transformation—both in his native US and in the UK. 'The first factor is the raw numbers—four in ten births out of wedlock now compared to a rate in the single digits as late as the 1970s. You've had a revolution in the UK. The second shift has been the move to talking about the two-parent family as just one of many equally valid alternatives. There is great resistance to talking about the merits of the two-parent family.'

Ultimately, he considers political correctness as having made the two-parent family a taboo topic. 'In the US I think that the root of this reluctance to talk about the two-parent family lies in the issue of race in the 1960s when civil rights was at its height. It fundamentally restricted our ability to talk about issues whenever the problem seemed to be most prevalent among blacks. Out-of-wedlock births was a prime example, because the percentage of black out-of-wedlock birth was much higher than the percentage for whites. I think some of that was happening here in the UK too. You risked being branded a racist if you criticised out-of-wedlock births, and nobody wants to be a racist.'

And so, he believes, we stopped talking about ideal parenting scenarios. 'In this climate of non-judgementalism it became impossible to talk about the hierarchy of family structures, that the two-parent family is better than the alternatives on a number of criteria involving the welfare of children.'

Murray sees single parenthood as being problematic by definition. 'What the Left will never be able to do is to accept that fathers play an irreplaceable role. Although many lone parents do very well, it is inherently problematic for large numbers of boys to grow up without fathers, and we need to accept that.'

To affect family life for the better, Murray argues, we need to stop subsidising single parenthood. 'The only way to get the preferred social arrangements is by stigmatising some alternatives and rewarding others. With lone parenthood, we need to ask "Is there a price?" And if a policy is softening that price, the policy needs to be changed. The only way to restore the two-parent family, the preferable context, is if lone parenthood carries economic consequences.

'You don't have to set up a bureau for penalising single women,' says Murray. 'A single woman trying to support herself and a baby faces all sorts of economic penalties as a matter of course. All that policy has to do is refrain from lifting those penalties.'

To an extent this withdrawal has been happening in the US, with Clinton's welfare reforms. Murray considers this to have had a beneficial impact, though he points out that the reform did not actually end support for single mothers. 'The rhetoric in the run-up to the reforms was much more draconian than the actual content of the reforms. The Left was so dramatic about the potential consequences of the changes in the welfare rules that it inadvertently helped the reforms to work—the Left scared many welfare recipients into getting jobs. Apart from that, there was a lot less resistance among welfare recipients than people had anticipated. Most people were fairly responsive to the idea that going out and getting a job is the right thing to do.'

Murray expresses his irritation with what he sees as the hypocrisy of the American Left. 'The first great hypocrisy is to say that families come in all shapes and sizes: they don't. Living arrangements do, but when they use the word "family" they are playing games with the English language. The second hypocrisy is the difference between what middle-class members of the Left say and what they do. The Left says "lone women raising children on their own is fine for other people, and it is unfair to criticise them". But when it comes to their own children, the great majority of members of the American Left who are part of the middle class just happen to end up raising their children in the traditional two-parent family. It's a form of condescension toward poor people—"it's okay for them, but it's not good enough for us".'

Unlike some conservatives, however, Murray is strongly against the notion of encouraging marriage through fiscal incentives. 'Good marriages do not result from people getting paid to get married. On the contrary. Paying people to get married will have precisely the opposite effect from the one you want. You want people to get married expecting to have to rely on each other to make an economic success of it. You want women to weigh whether the man will be an asset, and give preference to men who look like they will be good providers. Fifty years ago the question women asked was "will this man be someone I can depend upon?" The woman had to focus on that because she was the one left holding the baby if the man ran out on her. If the man didn't look like a good bet, she not only didn't marry him, she didn't let him sleep with her. Getting regular sexual access to a woman meant that a guy had to meet her demands, and those demands included acting like a good husband and father. The truth is that men respond to the demands that women make on them. It may not be fair, but it's a fact. If women want men to behave responsibly, they're going to have stop letting them off the hook. I don't know how to change the demands that women make on men, but until they do, not much will change.'

The bottom line, argues Murray, is that we should all be more careful when it comes to having babies. 'Bringing a child into the world is one of the most profoundly important things human beings do. The decision to do that should also be one of the most solemnly and carefully considered decisions we make. And too often it isn't.'

Michael Lamb
Developmental psychologist

Professor Michael Lamb is a developmental psychologist at Cambridge University. His main areas of research are social and emotional development, specifically in infancy and early childhood.

For Michael Lamb it is ultimately standards not structures which matter in families. 'It is the quality of parenting which is important, rather than the formal family structure. Whether parental separation affects children's adjustment depends on a number of factors; the sheer transition or change in structure itself is not important. The bulk of the evidence suggests that children do better when they have both parents actively involved in their lives. But the important thing is that children have meaningful relationships with both parents whether they live together or not. In this respect, family structure is less important than parental involvement.'

A clear improvement today, Lamb argues, is that fewer children today are alienated from their absent parents. 'Many kids today have a supportive relationship with their fathers. I think what public policy needs to explore is how to foster these relationships.

'When it comes to adolescence, children are especially affected by ineffective or absent parents. It is so important that the absent parent has a parenting, rather than just a "visiting uncle" role in the child's life. The quality of the relationship with the child suffers if contact and the context of this contact is limited. In these situations the relationship does tend to deteriorate over time. When a father is a visiting uncle rather than a dad the relationship loses its centrality and the potential benefits of parental involvement are squandered.

'It is vital that the absent parent disciplines and makes decisions about the child, for example doing their homework with her or him. In other words that the father is involved in the child's everyday life. Spending the night with their absent parent in the week, on school nights, for example. Being the "fun" parent, seen at the weekend, and the treat-giver, seems more fun for the child in the short-term but it adversely affects the quality of the relationship in the long-term. When the child hits 15, fun with dad is not going to be able to compete with girls and shopping, and a father who hasn't assumed a full paternal role will no longer be valued or needed.'

Lamb acknowledges that maintaining the quality of child/absent-father relationships is difficult. 'It is a tough challenge because children need to spend time in both their parents' homes; younger children in particular need over-nights at both parents. But although the whole process is very awkward, parents who don't have these arrangements in place are at a disadvantage. It is very important that the absent parent's time with the child spans school days so that they can get to know the child's school friends and do homework with them and are involved in discipline and limit-setting.'

It is also very important, Lamb argues, that stepparents are involved with their stepchildren. 'I think that stepparents can be a bonus. In some situations, stepparents feel uncertain about what their role should be. But ducking out is a bad solution. Stepparents need to be respected as authority figures.'

Parental gender, on the other hand, he thinks may not be as important as first thought. 'My view over time has changed a lot on this. In the 1970s the focus was on the differences between the roles of mothers and fathers—this was seen as important. But over time, data show that the gender of the parent is actually very unimportant. The important part of parenting has to do with sensitivity and the degree of commitment rather than aspects of masculinity and femininity. Gender in parenting has become a very politically charged issue relating to legislation to do with gay and single-parent adoption. But ultimately we've learned enough about gender to know that it's not significant in parenting.'

When it comes to single parenting, Lamb considers there to be a multitude of considerations. 'It is a big mistake to argue that it is all about economics. There are four ways that parental break-up affects children: one, economic; two, the quality of the relationship with the resident parent; three, the quality of the relationship with the non-resident parent; and four exposure to marital conflict.

'It is very difficult to say which of these factors is the most important. Many kids raised by single parents do just fine—it is a risk factor, but it is not deterministic. On balance children are going to do better if they have relationships with both of their parents. But we should not prescribe family structure on this basis, particularly because those relationships can be supportive whether or not the parents live together.'

Divorcing parents, Lamb emphasises, need to be very sensitive to their children's response. 'The last thing children need in this situation is to be faced with loyalty conflict—it's not healthy. It is fundamentally important that parents say, "we are getting divorced from each other but not from you".'

Professor Lamb is clear on what he sees as government policy's priority. 'The central thing in terms of children's long-term welfare is good, strong, supported and committed relationships with both parents. Therefore it is crucial that the goal of government policy is doing things that promote the possibility of committed parental investment in children.'

New Labour policy, Lamb believes, is progressing policy along the right lines. 'This government has made steps in the right direction. It is important to make it possible for parents to spend significant amounts of time in the early years with their children and parental leave policies are key to this. The government has made strides in the right direction to bring England closer to Europe on maternity leave rights. When it comes to paternity leave and rights the UK is, however, far behind—although the rhetoric is increasingly there.'

Nevertheless, the New Labour government is elevating the role of fathers, Lamb argues. 'I know that the Department of Health has recently recognised the importance of fathers' roles and responsibility. They have found that the best time to engage fathers is when the couple are pregnant, a time when fathers are most interested and can best be hooked in.

'The new rhetoric around the revised role of the Child Support Agency is also positive. There's now more focus on the child's relationship with their father after parental separation, rather than simply seeing the non-resident parent as a source of money—although that's certainly important too. In the past so much emphasis was placed on money that the importance of psychological ties was lost. The new tenor is reflected in the latest white paper.'[1]

He sees New Labour's concentration on children's early life chances as encouraging, but the strategies themselves sometimes flawed. 'The emphasis on investment in the early years, on Sure Start for example, is very positive. But a lot of money here has been squandered, a lot of investment hasn't been properly directed. The government in general has not been focused enough on the importance of quality in child care.

'Expenditure on child care in the UK compares poorly to the EU average. One of the reasons for this is because we're putting a lot of money into other activities. With Sure Start, for example, money is also being put into things other than child care. This government has embraced the importance of joined-up thinking, which is very beneficial; I applaud the creation of Children's Centres, for example. But I feel that there is not as much action on the ground as there is rhetoric, when it comes to these joined-up services.

'This government has been characterised by lots of good ideas but also not bedding those ideas in. So there've been lots of new initiatives, and flux, which has been quite demoralising for employees and agencies trying to keep up with these initiatives. Mandates keep changing, resources aren't there and employees are left dealing with a barrage of directives which don't help them think in a joined-up way. I also think that there is not enough middle-level management, only central management from the top. I think this government has made really important strides and identified important goals—but it needs to bed them in and follow them through.'

When it comes to Conservative policy, Lamb welcomes the noises that they have made so far. 'It's great to see a focus on child welfare from the Conservatives. But I haven't seen any clarity on how they would translate this rhetoric into action on the ground. I would hope—and I don't mean this cynically, I just don't know—it would build on these positive strides by providing more support and backbone to childcare services.'

Terri Apter
Social psychologist

Dr Terri Apter is a social psychologist at Cambridge University. Her areas of interest include the development of adolescents and young adults within the family and society, the changing balance of work and family in women's lives and mother/daughter relationships.

Terri Apter thinks families are presented with a number of dilemmas today, juggling work and childcare being one of the greatest. 'There have been a lot of changes in society affecting the family, and many of these are out of synch with working patterns. I think that there was an expectation that there would be more community childcare for one, but as more women are working there has actually been a decline in informal childcare, as well as a decline in social capital.

'There was also an expectation that working hours would be reduced, generally, and that has not happened. Employers still expect an employee to be able to work as though someone else were servicing her family life, day to day. Flexible working legislation is a step forward, but the culture of long hours and of showing a presence at work remains strong.'

Another challenge, Apter argues, is that children have become more time-consuming than ever before. 'Children these days seem to require more input. Conflated dangers, real or perceived, have put increased pressure on parents and on families, and working women in particular.'

Apter connects this to increasing rates of childlessness in the UK. 'What is related is the number of educated women having children. Out of those women born in the 1950s, 24 per cent of women were without children by the time they were in their forties; of those born in the 1970s, on the other hand, about 40 per cent will go into their forties childless. This trend is a real indication of how high women count the cost of childcare.

'The cost for women, if you look at lifetime earnings, of having children is high, and these costs are factored into decisions about having children. The value of caring labour in our society is low. There is a rhetoric endorsing its value, but no market reward.'

She feels that policy could be smarter on the issues around childcare. 'I have some sympathy for the government's initiatives, like Sure Start, for example. I sympathise with the aim of encouraging a competent population, and focusing on early education. I can see the benefits of getting women into the workplace to increase their human capital. But that does accept that caring for children isn't an economic activity and I think that is misguided. Not only people who engage in caring for children, but also those caring for elderly relatives, save the state an enormous amount.'

When it comes to gender equality in childcare, Apter considers that there is still a long way to go. 'Men's involvement in childcare is nowhere near comparable to women's involvement in the labour force. Part of the reason for this is that men's careers don't take into account what caring for a child involves.'

Like many, she looks to Scandinavia as a role model for fostering better equality. 'The Scandinavian countries are very good at keeping women in the workplace by providing good childcare. So there isn't the same tension between the stay-at-home mums and working mums, there isn't the "mummy wars" phenomenon. But there is still a gender division in Scandinavia in types of work, and still a gender division in caring in the home. It still has to be explained to men that the home help is there to look after the baby, not them!'

Apter sees a reversion to gender divisions as often coinciding with the arrival of children. 'Clearly before people have children there is a much more equal division of labour. But that does not seem to continue with childcare and an increase in tasks. Part of the reason may be that women just seem to respond more quickly to the needs of a child.'

Apter is ambivalent about children's own experience of childhood. 'It's very difficult to measure. In previous generations children had a horrible time. So rather than confusing some falsely idyllic time—and I don't know when that would be—we need to think about what we are doing to make it better.'

She sees some of the newer stresses children are experiencing as deriving from good intentions. 'A lot of the problem is that we do lots of silly, counterproductive things with good aims—and the government follows. Like the need to assess in education, which has resulted in over-tested, stressed-out children.

'Similarly with adolescents; there's a myth that in order to be mature teens have to be independent. Parents don't feel they should help them make decisions, but when facing professional and educational choices which are so complex it is actually very difficult to make choices—although parents can also take too much of a role, so we need to be careful about that.'

Ultimately, Apter considers today's working arrangements as hard to reconcile with parenting. 'With increased hours at work, being available for children is difficult. People talk about flexi-time but there is still a sense that being a good worker is being around all the time, sending emails in the middle of the night, that kind of thing. You just can't schedule quality time, you have to be responsive. And continuity is also very important—not just for very young children but for teens too.'

Apter is comfortable talking about preferable family structures—but she doesn't see a focus on structure as useful to policy-making. 'You can make generalisations about ideal scenarios. Over and over again it is found that young people who have a mother and a father do better—and that divorce is really tough on people. But I'm not sure government policy can do much to keep parents together. I think that it is a waste of time to say to a policy maker "you have to preserve the sanctity of the family". These changes in family structure are demographic trends and they're not going to stop there.

'However, it seems nonsensical to talk up the value of a two-parent family, and then have a tax structure that presents a disincentive to living as a couple. And that's how tax is currently structured.'

Although she thinks that New Labour's priorities for child welfare are right, Apter questions some of their strategies for achieving them. 'I think they meddle too much and that they change too many things too often. I also think they spend too much time engaged in focus groups instead of looking at "normal" people. They also tend to start with big ideas, which often lead to disjointed policies.'

Whether government policy can affect it or not, Apter does think that parental separation is an issue. 'It is problematic because there are many difficult consequences of a family breaking down.'

Susie Orbach
Psychoanalyst

Professor Susie Orbach is a psychoanalyst and feminist pioneer. She is author of Fat Is a Feminist Issue *and currently a Visiting Professor at the London School of Economics.*

Marriage is relevant today albeit fundamentally different from in the past, argues Susie Orbach. 'I'm sure that marriage has not gone away as an issue. But girls' identity is not caught up with marriage in the way that it used to be.'

In particular, she sees the dynamics of marriage as having changed. 'The changes in relationships today are to do with a stronger emphasis on partnership between men and women, and a move away from women providing all the dependency needs for men while men provide economic dependency. However the symbolism in marriage—the ceremonies, hen nights, the white dress—has increased. What this shows is that historical femininity is still intact.

'The white wedding aspiration can be explained by the fact that in late modernity we have a multiple of identities, we no longer have to choose *one*. A superficial parallel might be that girls now wear a frilly skirt with a pair of combat boots.'

She regards former preconceptions about marriage as no longer applicable. 'We can't make those assumptions anymore. Cohabiting relationships can involve gender inequity too. It's not about the "certificate" it's about the living together bit and the quality of the relationship.'

When it comes to parenting equality between men and women, Orbach sees progress—but also room for more. 'Inequality still exists in relationships although there is more equality; emotional labour still falls on women and there is structural inequality. Women need to make sure that all their family's needs are taken care of, they need to maintain the stability. This can be transferred, it's not an inherently female role. The trouble is that there aren't really internal models for this to follow so that it can become a male role.'

She believes that parenting equality does, however, lie within reach. 'It needn't be utopian, in Scandinavia private and social structures have managed to accommodate equality.'

Orbach sees looking after children as compatible with new expectations. 'Childcare can be very rewarding and stimulating. Work structures are currently not sufficiently flexible to accommodate gradual maternal re-entry. Children can be very engaging and a child "bond" is definitely not female specific. Breast-feeding is practical and emotional and it obviously creates a specific relationship between a mother and her baby; however, men can also make very specific or special relationships with their babies. The shape of the bonds may be different but they need not be less significant.'

Government policy has an important role to play in the family she argues. 'It is legitimate for the government to intervene, for example by saying that teen pregnancy is not usually positive: those that still need parenting should not be parenting themselves and government might take advice so it understands the emotional reasons that girls seek to have their own babies so young.'

However, not all forms of government policy are welcome. 'Rather than taking a fiscal or moral approach to determining social policy we should look at it from different angles. We need to take an approach other than moralising to talking about family structure. We need to look at what parenting is best for children, how that can happen, and therefore stability should be the focus, not necessarily marriage.'

Orbach believes that where state intervention can really help families is with work/life policies. 'In the workplace it is legitimate for the government to intervene to allow for more flexibility for childcare. Many women discover that they want to spend more time with their children than they'd thought they would. The reason this doesn't happen to men is probably because they spend less time with them — they are not exposed to the possibility of the situation.'

Linda Papadopoulos
Psychologist

Dr Linda Papadopoulos is a chartered psychologist. A household name through her psychological analysis on popular television shows, she is also a Reader in Psychology at London Metropolitan University.

Although Linda Papadopoulos thinks that young couples today have more freedoms than in the past, she believes that times haven't completely changed. 'I think there are lots of differences and lots of similarities. The differences centre on the freedoms now available to young couples with fewer gender stereotypes: women working, men looking after the children, and people having sex younger, for example. But at the same time, lots of pressures exist with trying to have something idyllic often based on former relationship forms, that years ago would have been conceived as "perfect".'

Papadopoulos considers relationships to have become more 'dispensable'. 'I think a key difficulty lies in the paradoxes of our expectations and aspirations. Because of the nature of our instant-gratification society, we think that if a relationship isn't reaching our expectations we can just throw it away. It's all about me, me, me and disposable relationships. But,' cautions Papadopoulos, 'I'm not suggesting that we need a Victorian "just put up with it" attitude either.'

She sees the positives in today's relationships as centring on greater autonomy. 'For example, the fact that divorce can now be seen as liberating rather than stigmatising. There is a problem however, and that is that people want this power in their personal lives—the power to leave, to be their happiest—but without the responsibility, say once children are involved. With freedom comes the complexity of choice.'

Papadopoulos points to the related fact that it is not simply a rise in divorces that we are now seeing, but a rise in the number of divorces *per person*. 'With relationships today, in a sense it's almost as though each one is a practising ground. So we wind up learning through a series of relationships rather than within one because we move on when we're unhappy in a relationship rather than working at it.'

She sees what she refers to as the 'urban family' as our new form of relationship support. 'The importance of the "urban family" today is why *Friends* did so well. We could recognise their set-up in our own lives. The difficulty is that our reliance on the urban family means that we don't get perspectives from other generations but just our girlfriends, and that is a loss. We don't see the experiences of other generations as relevant and therefore useful. I think that the problem here is that we see our families as something of the past. Once we've left them they are no longer relevant to our lives today. We think Mum wouldn't understand.'

Papadopoulos regards marriage as definitely still relevant, but the meaning dependent 'hugely on background'. 'For many people it's the difference between committing and not committing. For others it's almost like religion: you're Catholic, Protestant, but you don't question it—it's the same with marriage, you don't question it.'

She acknowledges however, that not everybody attaches value to getting married. 'For some people marriage *is* just a piece of paper, they are already connected. But having said that, I think that for many getting married is about having the courage to stand up for it because in the current climate there is a slight disdain for it.'

By this she means that marriage, in her view, is sometimes unfairly characterised. 'Marriage is sometimes seen to be patriarchal because it is an institution. But I don't see why an institution is a bad thing, it needn't be a negative at all. For a lot of women in the world marriage can be liberating in that it gives them freedoms and safety; for a lot of women marriage is about a contract.' For others, Papadopoulos argues, getting married has a significance beyond the practical. 'And for many people marriage is a very spiritual thing, the ultimate sign of their love for each other. A lot of people who write off marriage are missing these points. So to call marriage a patriarchal institution I think is a sweeping statement, it has a much deeper spiritual, and for some, practical, meaning.'

Having said that, Papadopoulos has reservations herself about what she refers to as the "Bridezilla phenomenon" in modern marriages. 'A lot of emphasis can be put on the wedding itself today. It's me, me, me—how pretty will my dress look, how curly will my hair be, that is what's significant, the focus—not the lifetime together. The trouble is we live in a game-show society where we want something for nothing—reality TV stars making millions for doing nothing. And this attitude is increasingly manifest in relationships. But actually a relationship needs nurture, like a plant.'

Papadopoulos perceives a definite difference in marital aspirations between the sexes. 'Women think about what they will gain, whereas men think about what they will lose.' Ultimately, she thinks women are keener to get married than men because they want children. 'It's the tick-tock of the biological clock and I think that women who think it's time to have children would rather do it with a partner. They think it would make more sense to not do it alone. Parenting is really hard work! It's going to be hugely difficult doing everything alone.'

As such, Papadopoulos sees single parents as having a tough job. 'Couple parenting is definitely preferable. A girlfriend of mine who recently divorced, said that the worst thing about it was looking after her baby alone. *That* is what was the most traumatic element, being solely responsible. This is not to say that many mothers on their own are not doing a great job, but that four hands and two heads is going to make it a lot easier.'

Papadopoulos also thinks that parenting in pairs is valuable in the sense of bringing different gender influences to children. 'You can socialise children until the cows come home but this will always be the case. This is not to say that men can't nurture and women work and so on, but that it is an evolutionary fact that there are differences. I think it is a mistake to try and deny this.'

There are also persisting differences between men and women in childcare patterns, Papadopoulos believes. 'Despite a lot of social change when it comes to men and women's roles, attitudes to parenting are much the same as they were. There are a number of reasons for this: there is room for women to have children and take time out of their careers and this is not frowned upon, whereas for men it is. Also, in the vast majority of countries men earn more. Then, there is a lot of peer pressure: try going back to work as a mum when your child is two months old—or try being a house-husband.'

Nevertheless, some progress has been made according to Papadopoulos. 'What *has* changed is the *type* of involvement men have in childcare now: it's alright for men to change nappies now.'

Jenni Murray
President of the Fawcett Society

Jenni Murray is presenter of Radio 4's Woman's Hour *and President of the Fawcett Society.*

Like many parents, Jenni Murray has had to face the work/parenting dilemma. 'We had a very good nanny for many years who enabled us both to work. After that we found it very difficult to find a good nanny, and we realised that one of us needed to be there. As children get older I think they need one parent around for intellectual input.'

It wouldn't be Murray staying at home, however, but her partner David. 'In my case, there was hardly any discussion about who should stay at home. David wasn't that bothered, so he was the one that stayed at home.'

She remembers that initially this was fairly difficult for him. 'It was the late 70s/early 80s and there were hardly any men at the school gates—as well as the fact that it coincided with the height of the paedophile scare! There were no networks for men, no coffee mornings and things like that, as there were for women.

'But it did get easier. We moved to the North and David found that there were other guys looking after the children. This had come about largely because of employment difficulties in the North—to do with redundancies in industries like mining—whereas there was still "women's work".'

Murray feels that today the involvement of fathers in childcare has begun to change, heralded by the formation the Fatherhood Institute (formerly Fathers Direct), the lobbying group founded by Duncan Fisher and Jack O'Sullivan. 'They lobbied for fathers involvement but they understood feminist perspectives and were interested in a family where both parents were involved in family life. There is much more boxing and coxing nowadays—although I'm sure this isn't countrywide. But amongst the *Woman's Hour* staff there's lots of boxing and coxing where both partners are going part-time, as well as finding ways of job-sharing.'

Murray sees several factors as having contributed to this shift, though the principle of equality is not necessarily one of them. 'Men have begun to understand how important psychological connections are with their children. Men want to be able to be more emotional and more involved. But where there is actual equality in parenting it tends to be by happy coincidence.'

Murray believes it is important that mothers and fathers are equally involved, but that parenting shouldn't revolve around gender. 'We need to be really careful about gender stereotyping in parenting. My son Ed, for example, would rather jump off the Eiffel Tower than put on a pair of rugby boots. But he used to love going riding with me—a girly sport. But Charlie, my other son, loves going shopping on Bond Street—although he also loves going to rugby matches with his dad.'

In her own childhood, Murray remembers doing a great variety of activities. 'I, on the other hand, was an only child and did both "girly" and "guy stuff". As a child I used to sit in the kitchen and watch my mother cook but I also wanted to go out to work. I think it's important to be careful about gendered activities: don't push children into boxes of masculinity and femininity.'

Murray sees legislation as crucial to supporting parenting equality between mothers and fathers. She mentions the Scandinavian examples. 'There, fathers *have* to take all their paternal leave or they lose the right to it and many more do take it and are very happy. In this country a man has to sacrifice pay to take paternity leave and very few men are in the position to do that.'

Having said that, Murray believes that when it comes to parenting choice is vital. 'Looking after my children was never something that I desired to do—I would have hated being at home all day and I'm hopeless in the kitchen. But I have a very good relationship with my sons—I go out to dinner with the one who is at university in London about once a fortnight.'

'What we want is that women can make true choices. If a woman genuinely wants to look after her children, then that is a true choice—but we equally don't want to condemn women for choosing to work. In my case abandoning them as soon as I could! Had the baby on the Friday/Saturday, and was back at work on the Monday. I couldn't get back to work quick enough.'

Murray points out, however, that a big hurdle to *real* choice is who the main breadwinner is. 'It tends to be the male, and that's key in the decision-making about who goes back to work.'

On the topic of cohabitation, Murray thinks we should look twice at the trends. 'We need to be very careful when we interpret cohabitation statistics because what never emerges from the statistics are the two types of cohabitation: committed cohabitation and what I call "bunking up for a year or two". I, for example, cohabited in a totally committed relationship. I stayed unmarried for political reasons: I didn't want to enter into the patriarchal institution. I *did* get married two years ago for inheritance tax purposes. I did also get married when I was younger,' Murray adds, 'but that was for convenience's sake—my mother would have killed me if I'd lived with my boyfriend.'

Ultimately, Murray sees marriage as irredeemably patriarchal. 'You are still asked for your father's name on the marriage certificate, but when I asked 'what about my mother's name?' they said that that wasn't necessary. Women are still written out of history. I think that a lot of women don't want to enter into such an institution.'

For those who want to marry, fine, says Murray, but she would prefer heterosexuals to be given the choice of making a civil partnership 'which carries none of the historical baggage of marriage'. 'I am very cross that we have not got civil partnership rights for heterosexuals. It's discrimination against heterosexuals that homosexuals can have them and heterosexuals can't.' As important as taking the chauvinism out of relationships is taking off the rose-tinted spectacles, Murray argues. Our failure to do so, she thinks, explains today's higher rates of relationship dissolution. 'We raise our kids with romantic notions that it's going to be happily ever after. We don't ever tell our children that it is like a business relationship—it needs to be treated like a business relationship. It's a very long commitment.'

This matters particularly, says Murray, because parental separation is so hard on children. 'You owe it to your kids to stay together—although get out of course if there's violence—but for any other reason, stay together. I think parental separation is a failure; when couples split up they perform an enormously immoral act. But when it comes to couples without children,' Murray adds, 'I couldn't give a damn, they can do what they like.'

Murray has mixed views on New Labour's family record. 'Labour has half got it right in the way that it has supported those needing support, but it's got to the point now where they're saying 'we can't afford to pay for you actually'. If it were up to me we would be putting money into care for the elderly; I've got first-hand experience of the crisis this is in today.'

The Conservatives, Murray argues, certainly don't have a better record. 'I'm coming from a very mature feminist viewpoint. Compare the treatment of unmarried women now with the past. Unmarried mothers were social pariahs or were heartbroken if they did the then right thing and had the child adopted. So I do have sympathy for women who become lone parents, but less sympathy than I would have had 50 years ago. With good access to contraception and early terminations, I cannot see many reasons—apart from violence—for women to become lone parents. In any other circumstances, well maybe you should have taken the pill or perhaps considered a termination.

'The trouble is that the Conservative Party never went through that middle stage—I mean remember that Peter Lilley "I have a little list" speech? Their approach was so *punitive*. We're not going to punish women for these mistakes,' says Murray in conclusion, 'but equally, you made your bed, you really ought to be grown up enough to lie in it.'

Jenny Watson
Chair of the Equal Opportunities Commission

Jenny Watson is an Associate with Global Partners and Associates and a co-author of the Human Rights Act Toolkit. *At the time of interview she was Chair of the Equal Opportunities Commission.*

Jenny Watson has witnessed several governments as Chair of the Equal Opportunities Commission (EOC): 'Whilst I think that governments have a significant impact on the quality of family life, I believe that people will of course always make the decisions that are right for their family—that they don't allow government to dictate their behaviour. Regardless of policy, people will live their lives no matter what. We are witnessing a major change in the structure of the family.

'I wouldn't say that there is a perfect family,' Watson says, but she does think we can learn from abroad, from the Mediterranean family for example. 'Children are much more involved in public life than here. There is much more involvement in public space. The idea that the family, as a unit, goes out in the evening together, look at Greece, Spain, Italy, this is an alien concept here. There is a very different concept there about family and community, and grandparents are more involved.'

Watson has however noticed a significant increase in grandparent involvement in childcare in the UK. 'There is a different concept of the extended family emerging with grandparents being more engaged now. Particularly over the school holidays.'

A constraint to this, she notes, is that many younger grandmothers have to work. 'The government needs perhaps to give more recognition to informal childcare,' she argues, alluding to the possibility of subsidising care.

Attitudes to fatherhood, she says, are also shifting. 'For one, women's expectations are very clear. The EOC's research also shows that fathers are very keen to be more involved.'

Similarly, Watson argues that the number of fathers who alter their working hours after the birth of children is now 'quite high', and the take-up of flexible working hours also on the up. 'There has been a shift from about 11 per cent to 31 per cent in less than five years between 2002 and 2005.'

But men being the primary carer continues to be a fairly novel concept in the UK, Watson adds. 'I think it is still a brave thing to do to acknowledge that as a father you will take a substantial share of the childcare, a bit like coming out at work.'

That mothers continue to do the bulk of childcare, she says, is a lot to do with economics. 'I can imagine a situation where a couple are having a baby and the question will be asked, 'who will give up their job for childcare?' With the pay gap, logically it is not going to make sense to sacrifice the higher salary.'

In this respect, Watson sees the disparity between men and women's wages as negative for men as well as women. 'The pay gap constrains men's choices. The difficulty is that the way that the leave is structured it is perceived as a woman's leave. Redressing this poses a challenge for the government.'

Something which Watson thinks is long due in the UK is transferable parental leave. 'The UK has had one of the most unequal systems of leave in Europe for some time. In other words, there is a lot of catching up to do with attitude, rather than vice versa. Again, men's choices are constrained by the fact that maternity leave is not entirely transferable.'

Furthermore, she argues, transferable leave would help women's prospects in the workplace. 'That way, women would face less discrimination. Indeed with the right to request leave being extended to carers, many of whom are men who work, this already changes the situation for employers.'

EOC research shows that men appear to be keen on the idea. 'The research shows that far more of the fathers said yes to taking up the transferable maternity leave than the mothers did to the fathers' taking it up.'

Watson believes that choice is what matters when it comes to division of labour. 'I find the current media debate on this very frustrating: if you are a mother and you go to work you feel guilty; if you stay at home you feel guilty.'

Flexibility in the workplace is something Watson sees as both contributing to choice and on the up. 'The employer does increasingly see the benefits of flexible working. There are practical benefits to accommodating flexibility, such as smaller offices in the case of working from home. The best employers will consider flexible working if there is a business case which can be met, and new start-up businesses invariably adopt flexible working.'

Watson can however see that flexible working is not a panacea when it comes to work/life balance. 'You could never say that every job could be done flexibly.' Moreover, ignorance of rights is also narrowing the scope of flexible working patterns. 'At the moment, the only people who have a legal right to ask for flexible hours are parents with children under six. And EOC research shows that there was much ignorance amongst carers about this right.'

An issue which Watson predicts will soon top the family policy agenda is caring for family members other than children. 'Caring, generally for parents, is going to become a very consuming challenge and will become a very big debate. The number of carers is increasing. The thing about carers is that there is often no choice. The caring issue has significant implications for family policy. Unlike childcare, there is no predictability. This is a big issue to do with the family.'

Overall, Watson sees a distinct political divide when it comes to family policy. 'In my personal view, the political Left came at the issue of families very much from a perspective of women's equality—which was the right thing to do at the time, and given the history of the labour movement probably inevitable. Women hadn't always found it easy to be heard and there was ground to make up.

'At the same time the Right was having a debate about "families" which consisted often in the public sphere of defining the shape of the family, best encapsulated for many around the whole "Back to Basics" campaign. As David Cameron himself has said, that wasn't always a nice debate, particularly the part of the debate about lone parents. It was often judgemental. And it wasn't about providing support to families, rather about saying "this is the right way to live your life as a family", don't expect support from us if you choose not to take this route, the state is not going to pick up the pieces for people's "lifestyle choices".'

Watson thinks both sides of the political divide have since been on a journey. 'The Left moved from women's rights to a debate about child poverty, and now a mature debate about how men and women work together to manage work and home. It is now firmly claiming the territory of supporting families with an increasingly prominent role for fathers right from the time a child is born.'

She sees the Right as being somewhat in a state of flux on the family. 'I'm not sure that debate on what might broadly be called the Right, or indeed within the Conservative party, has yet reached a settled position: there is still strong support for marriage and "full-time mothers" as the "correct" approach from some interest groups, and a push for a more modern approach based on a wider range of choices from others. David Cameron's policy of providing tax breaks for couples who are married or in a civil partnership so that one partner, usually the woman, can stay at home with the children, flies in the face of public opinion. Our polling shows two thirds of people think support should go to families in their broadest sense, not be restricted to only a sub-set.'

Watson sees marriage as 'a matter of personal choice' and is adamant that policy should not privilege it. 'If you want a policy that benefits children, it is crucial that you don't have a policy that benefits the decision of the parents, and therefore penalises some children, because for example, the parents did not get married. The commitment should be to support parenting for every parent.'

Watson points to what she perceives as the weaknesses in the Conservative's proposals on marriage incentives. 'It fails to provide very much for families in which both parents work, and it fails to tackle the root of the problem which is to make our society, including our workplaces, more family friendly though of course their welcome proposals on flexible working do try to address this issue. It also fails to reach the 40 per cent of children who are born every year outside marriage. There is a risk that it will be portrayed as "Back to Basics II".'

The EOC wonders whether the Conservatives can continue to be the 'party of the family': they publicly debated this issue with David Cameron shortly after he took over the party leadership. 'Labour has done so much for the family, for example through Sure Start and tackling child poverty. I think it is possible to say that the Left approached the family issue from the perspective of women. Now they have moved towards the family.'

This shift on the Left she sees as having come about through necessity. 'Parties are aware that they need to respond to people's lives. They need to negotiate work and family and new assumptions about gender equity. This has meant changes to the debate.'

As to whether single parenting, a concern associated with the Right, should be problematised by the government, Watson believes we need to look at the underlying factors. 'Most people who have children are in a relationship when they have a child. Something happens around family support when the relationship between the parents breaks up. When children are born the expectation is that they, the parents, will have looked after the child together, and something happens.'

Again work/life balance is relevant, Watson argues. 'How can you enable parents to look after children and keep their relationship going? Work/life balance is relevant to healthy relationships, between both parents, and parents and children. What I don't consider to be useful here, in supporting families, is saying "you should get married". I think things like Sure Start's parenting skills support is helpful.'

Watson has found the old-fashioned debate around fathers, resident or non-resident, very frustrating, 'because their role in families was never clear: it was just "families need fathers". The newer debate, around the role that fathers should play in the family, is much healthier. We know that fathers have a hugely beneficial impact on the child, and it's very difficult bringing up a child on your own, it's knackering!'

Watson does think that there is 'more room' for relationship support from the government—both whilst parents are together and if they split. 'I think that support is necessary—relationship support if things start to go wrong, but not with the aim of forcing people to stay together. In the case of violence, support can be to help someone leave a relationship.' Ultimately, however, Watson considers the most important relationship to be the parenting one. 'The one between parents and child. Policy could be better at supporting both parents' relationships with their children when they split up. Flexibility could be critical to enabling both parents to spend time with their children.'

Watson refers to research by the EOC showing that seven in ten people are worried about what life will be like for their children and grandchildren; in particular because of work pressures. 'We are in a period of social revolution. We think that the social revolution started and ended in the swinging sixties, but actually it started in the 1930s and we're still going through it. The world of work has not caught up with that change.'

Polly Toynbee
Social commentator

Polly Toynbee is a columnist for the Guardian *and author of* Hard Work: Life in Low-Pay Britain.

Polly Toynbee sees the family as having undergone significant change, with one particularly striking outcome. 'The single biggest change is single parenthood. Mostly through divorce and separation a seismic shift has occurred. A big problem is that we're left in a society with a half-made revolution: economically we still require two parents—women cannot manage to survive alone in today's structures. So lone parenthood is mostly a recipe for terrible poverty. Economically I agree with the Right about family breakdown being a problem, but only because of the way society has failed to adapt to the changing shape of family life.'

Toynbee is less in agreement about their policies however. 'The Right always say that we must prevent family break-up, but their solutions, tax incentives for married couples, would be a miniscule amount of money to achieve huge attitude change. You cannot change behaviour simply through minor tax bribes. Divorce is already an economic disaster for most couples and yet people still do it. People live as they want, regardless of the high cost which ought to be a far greater financial deterrent than a small tax benefit.'

As Toynbee sees it, there is nothing that could be done in a democracy to prevent parental separation. 'The Tories would have to do something really drastic like cut lone-parent benefits altogether. That way you might get women looked after by the men. But to have any true effect, policies would have to be very draconian, leaving women and children to starve: I can't imagine that any party would get voted in with such policies. You would have to wave an axe over their heads in order to prevent family break-up.'

Her main objection to the Conservatives' ideas on tackling parental separation is that they are accompanied by 'bogus policies'. 'It's fiddlesticks that their policies would actually have the desired effect.

I'm open to solutions for preventing family breakdown, if someone came up with a good formula. But no one is coming up with any.'

The government, Toynbee thinks, has managed to be somewhat more practical when it comes to single parents. 'Labour has brought in childcare for the first time. At least this makes it more probable that more single mothers will work—and many more are now working, if not yet enough. But terrible poverty is still a reality for many single parents today. This is going to be the case as long as women's earnings are low, as long as women's labour is poorly paid—the four c's: catering, childcare, cash registers and cleaning. We have to revalue the jobs at the bottom, the traditionally female jobs.'

She also sees the worth—or lack of—attached to childcare as a related problem. 'Childcare is not seen as valuable, and both in and outside the home it's paid rottenly. One of the problems with female employment generally is that there is still a perception that women are doing jobs for "pin money".

'It's all about female inequality,' she concludes. 'All the new freedom that has been granted to women is the freedom to starve: it's the half-made revolution.'

Toynbee considers irresponsible fathers to be an urgent issue, and central to the difficulties faced by single parents. 'The Child Support Agency (CSA) raises a whole other problem: the whole-scale rebellion of fathers not willing to pay for their children. It seems that no laws have remedied this problem: when people en masse refuse to pay a tax, or in this case child maintenance, the state is pretty powerless. If errant fathers did pay up, single mothers would be much better off. But the government is giving up on the CSA and trying something new: it won't work unless there is a social attitude change among men and fathers are shamed into paying.'

Toynbee suggests that the government might instead pay the child support to mothers and then take it off the fathers. 'That way the state would take the hit. The problem with that though would be that there would then be no guilt factor for errant fathers as they would know that the state was paying. It would be hard to recoup the cash—but it could be taken at source and mothers would get their due.'

Socio-economic class is something Toynbee sees as highly relevant in relation to parental separation. 'I don't think that class has been taken enough into account. In the case of divorce, for example, the richer you are, the less likely you are to divorce.' She ponders on why this might be the case: 'Perhaps because the richer you are the more you have to lose, or perhaps richer people turn a blind eye to infidelity or have a "deal". You have the space to live separate lives—and you don't have the rows about money that happen in poor families where fathers keep more than they should from the housekeeping.

'There are common illusions, for example, about divorce. You are more likely to be divorced if you are poor, which isn't very surprising as money rows are one of the commonest causes of divorce. I suppose, considering the strain of being poor, that there is no incentive to be together, they may even gain a bit by splitting up. I do doubt though that people actually split up to get benefits. Most women would prefer to have a man around—so long as he doesn't take money that should be for children. I think that the Right's moralising agenda on this is particularly problematic: poor women throw out men if they are a drain and not a wage-earner for the family, to protect their children. For them, divorce is the right solution for their children—something the Right never mentions.'

Alongside the difficulties, Toynbee does see positives in parental separation today. 'Many people in the past had to have "shot-gun weddings" or a life sentence with someone who could be quite crazy or violent. One in four women suffer domestic violence at some time. Ability to escape is an essential freedom the Right rarely mentions.'

Ultimately, Toynbee thinks that we can talk about preferable parenting structures. 'Everybody thinks that a child's best upbringing is two happy parents—it's what people want. Yes, people sometimes abandon a partner for frivolous reasons, but it's unlikely that people split up lightly. Some men may flit, but women are mostly responsible.'

When it comes to having children, Toynbee sees marriage as still relevant. 'Marriage is still attached to legal things—houses, pensions… things that matter when you have children. I think if people don't have children it doesn't matter whether they are married. But I think that marriage may make children feel more secure.'

She thinks that we should be wary of drawing too many conclusions about marriage's effect however. 'Although marriage may be a sign of solidity I don't think that it actually creates solidity. For example, religion probably plays a role in marriage's stability because people who are religious are more likely to get married and are also less likely to get divorced, for religious reasons. I think that this factor tips the figures that say married couples stay together longer, hugely.

'There is a subtle difference between being married or not, but it is a marker for certain types of relationship—not a magic remedy that would transform less stable relationships,' she adds.

As to whether marriage has negative connotations, Toynbee feels that it does not. 'No, it's not inherently chauvinist or patriarchal as an institution, not really. Some people worry about it being patriarchal but I don't feel strongly about it. What I do feel strongly about is the glib way marriage is treated as a fix-all. And I think that the way people marry for frivolous expensive weddings is appalling.'

As she says, her real views give little support to the attacks of her critics. 'I'm really not the "crazy feminist" people like Melanie Philips think I am. The point of my type of feminism is how to get on with men—not how to get rid of them.'

Parenting, Toynbee thinks, is an area where more of this type of negotiation between men and women is necessary. 'There is still a great disparity in responsibility. Shared parenting is so important. The single most clinically depressed group are women at home alone with their young children. And I can see how this role has become even more lonely with more women at work.'

Toynbee sees the stay-at-home role as potentially dangerous for other reasons too. 'Men might bugger off, so it's absolutely imperative that women keep a toe in the labour market. Don't leave your job before you're established, in order to keep a working identity. Having to start all over again after years away from work is hard. Most women, I think, prefer a balance of work and childcare, though there are some who do want to stay at home.'

Toynbee acknowledges that there are many dilemmas around juggling parenting and work. 'Men tend to work hardest and the longest hours when children are very young: it's just a really unfortunate coincidence. The same is true for women: the time when they have children is a key make-or-break career time.'

She is adamant that more could be done in the workplace to help work/home life balance for parents, particularly through employment legislation. 'We could start by signing the 48-hour working agreement. There is also more room for part-time and flexi-time in the labour market. OK, the prime minister is not going to be able to work part-time, it won't obviously be possible in every job. But I do think that everybody should be able to have flexible hours. And I think it is necessary to make this statutory. We need to arrive at a situation where the employer is the one in law who needs to prove why you can't work from home.'

All advertised jobs, she argues, should also be advertised as potential job-shares. 'On the whole, unlike working-class jobs, middle-class jobs are not part-time. Employers would benefit too. They would get rather a good deal—two fresher employees. What I would really like to see is a scenario where employees did not loose seniority by going part-time, just pay.'

On the question of whether childhood is more difficult today, whether there are more pressures, Toynbee is sceptical. 'Every generation always thinks childhood has got worse, but I doubt it is more difficult today. I spent the whole time ferrying my children around to ballet, violin, and language classes. I don't think the classes made much difference—they don't speak French!—and they weren't necessary, but my children did enjoy them.'

In terms of hardship in childhood, Toynbee thinks that class plays an enormous role and therefore generalisations are useless. 'Drug and alcohol addiction, for example, tend to affect lower- not middle-class children—yet frequently the issues are posed as if affecting everybody.'

For lower-income children, Toynbee believes that the picture today is mixed. 'Things are worse in some respects, like acute social problems such as drug and alcohol addiction. But things have also got better in many ways for children—there has been a steady improvement of life chances under New Labour.'

Toynbee sees poverty as the ultimate problem for children, because so many problems stem from it. 'Things like not being able to afford school trips, going swimming, to the cinema or a birthday party which other children at school do. You can't underestimate the impact of poverty, and other adversities tend to follow.'

Caring allowances for parents, such as the APE[1] in France, she sees as unrealistic. 'The dead-weight cost would be such that it would be unsustainable. No government is going to pay people to do a job that they are already doing.

'I do think that it would make it better if mothers could stay at home for a whole year through longer paid maternity—and it would be wonderful to extend that to 18 months as in Sweden. However I can see that a danger of paying mothers to stay at home for years would be a great disincentive to work and that would mean more destitute women forced into dependency if the men left.'

When it comes to family policies, although Toynbee doesn't necessarily disagree with all the Conservative proposals in principle, she considers their tactics to be problematic. 'Every politician has said that the two-parent family is a good thing. But if a government has a little to spend, would you spend it on two-parent families who are mainly already better off or on one-parent families? I think that the Tories' economic analysis about lone parents plight is right, but the practical consequences of their marriage bonus policy would be wrong. It's the deeds, not the words, that matter. The Tories have made odd noises in terms of their policies. Keeping to this government's child poverty target, for example: it is mind-boggling how they will square it with lower spending over time.'

'The problem with Tory policy is that they do not think through the sharp corners. The argument between Left and Right is that the moralising on the Right is superficial: the reality of their policies is quite different. They never did do anything draconian in terms of tackling lone-parenthood, for example.'

Toynbee illustrates this with John Gummer's proposal of putting single mothers into institutions as a deterrent. 'Never mind the fact that this would actually have cost about £50,000 each a year, they didn't even trial anything of the sort. I can see where they were coming from though, the idea that making lone-parenthood this unappealing would dissuade people from lone-parenthood. But it was utterly unrealistic: voters would be appalled at putting deserted wives in a workhouse.'

Toynbee thinks that the Conservatives, and politicians more generally, would do well to introduce more realism. 'The Tories are under the illusion that government tax policy can change the culture. I think it is particularly odd that they think that, considering they are the small government, anti-nanny state party, and considering how little faith people have in politicians.

'I really do want politicians to be thought well of, but I think that they make the mistake of over-promising—like Blair for example. I think it would be more convincing if politicians were less absolutist. Politicians need to do less moralising and take a less grandiose approach.'

Nevertheless, overall Toynbee is impressed with New Labour's record on the family. 'New Labour has done amazingly well, nearly hitting the poverty targets, with childcare, with Sure Start for families, and tax credits. I do wonder, however, how New Labour is going to reach the 2010 child poverty target in time. Nevertheless, no government has done so much redistribution to poor children. Back in 1979 only one in seven children was poor. After the Conservative years, when Labour took over in 1997 it had shot up to one in three. It shows how hard this is to shift that Labour has only managed so far to improve this to one in four.'

Linda Bellos
Activist and campaigner

Linda Bellos is an activist and campaigner. She introduced Black History Month into the UK and was the first black member to join the feminist group Spare Rib.

Linda Bellos sees the family as vital for children—but thinks we need to widen our understanding of it. 'I'm a keen fan of the family—but it's very important that there are also alternative concepts to the simple understanding of family as parents and 2.4 children.'

In many ways, Bellos thinks that there is a healthier understanding of family abroad. 'In France and Greece, for example, children are an everyday and integral part of public life. There were two hindrances to this here: firstly the way in which the nuclear family is isolated from the rest of society and secondly, the importance we give to work. Children need a better role in society; at the moment they are pushed to the margins. I think that the emphasis on work also affects children's lives through the education system: all the emphasis on exams is about preparing children for the labour market.'

Policy-wise Bellos regards New Labour's record as generally impressive. 'It's been good overall: Sure Start, expanding nursery provision. I'm not suggesting that there isn't much more to do though, that they aren't desperately nanny-ish.'

Bellos sees a detachment from life on the ground as a central impediment to current policymaking. 'They really need to do a class analysis: people who sit around in Islington deciding what's best for those living in council houses might be a bit out of touch. Essentially we're talking about class: class is the elephant in the room in this conversation. To have the Islington set making decisions on family—although they aren't always entirely wrong—is problematic. Solutions need to come from communities, from grandparents and parents.'

Conservative policies, Bellos argues, are not concrete enough. 'There's been mood music and syrup with the Tories, but the party is not really offering any tangible changes.'

When it comes to difficulties faced by families, Bellos feels that work has become one of the greatest issues. 'Something which I think is a core problem for families, is "presenteeism"—just being at work for the sake of being at work. Arriving early and leaving late—although you're probably playing computer games half the day. This climate of being seen in the office is really important because it's such a problem for parents, especially working mums.'

Bellos' solution is simple: less time in the workplace. 'Everyone should work shorter hours. With, say, a 30-hour week both men and women would be more productive—and would be able to spend more time with their families.'

Furthermore, she sees a 30-hour week as achievable in this country. 'Norms can be changed—just as it was once a cultural norm to drink and drive. What is needed is a leadership model which is about the quality of what you do rather than the quantity.'

A work-related problem which Bellos feels strongly about is the desperate need to elevate the importance of childcare. 'It's completely undervalued. It's seen as women's work and therefore gets women's pay. We know it should be paid better. There would be a problem with that however, because then parents would find it difficult to afford childcare if carers were paid better—often an entire salary goes on childcare as it is.'

On the positive side, she thinks that men have become more involved in looking after children. 'In my daughter's household, for example, childcare is divided equally with her husband. In her case the extended family—the grandparents—are closely involved with childcare too. A mentality open to the idea of family not being restricted to the nuclear model actually makes this possible. If we keep the two parents, 2.4 children model, this isn't going to be possible.'

Talk about "ideal" scenarios isn't useful, Bellos argues. 'In an ideal world, every child is a wanted child. It's not necessarily having two parents because people won't always achieve that, for example if one of the parents dies. It's the *quality* of the model that matters and the state needs to support it whatever that model is. Judgements about models do not help: in the past women were put into institutions for having children unmarried. That's repellent and repugnant. Balance is important, not either or.'

Within this balance, marriage sits comfortably. 'Marriage is not a bad thing. These days, with other choices available, marriage may be good and other types of relationship more unequal for example.

'It's very clear that many men and women want to make a commitment. It is a fairly universal human desire. And look how much marriage has changed—for the better. The freedom to end it, if that is the right thing to do, is very important. Many will choose to marry, ideally the right person. But humans are prone to mistakes however.

'I have no problem with commitment—I think it's great for the individuals and great for society—and for children, without a doubt. But if it doesn't work it wouldn't make it easier on children if divorce were made harder. Look at the way that children are fought over as commodities, that's not good for them at all.'

When it comes to single parenting, Bellos has mixed views. 'The rate of poverty hasn't significantly changed, but being a single parent *may* exacerbate poverty. Women who have children without a partner should *not* be punished. There is an argument on the Right that if you support single parents you are encouraging it. I can see that there is an issue with single parenting, namely very young girls having children because they have low aspirations—and that issue of low aspirations absolutely needs to be addressed. On the other hand young women having children alone because they *want* to, that's not necessarily such a bad thing—especially biologically.'

However Bellos thinks that women parenting alone due to negligent fathers is not acceptable. 'Men behaving irresponsibly and having lots of children is not on. Having a child is a big responsibility, they should be aware of the responsibility. We have to persuade young men and women that you need to use contraception to have a child when you choose—and young men ought to recognise the responsibility of having children. But there are worse things in the world than raising a baby alone. It isn't inevitable that you will stay in poverty, there are many examples of single parents going on to be successful. If we gave more support to single parents—family, community support, grandparents and parents—they would be more able to work and get on in life.'

Bellos sees increases in relationship breakdown as both a sign of progress and problems. 'There are positives and negatives. It's very easy to get married, very easy indeed. I wonder whether people are getting married for the wrong reasons? I think—and I hope—that people are marrying for different reasons—marriage was once a prison. But the ease with which one can enter civil partnerships and marriage, which are meant to be for life, is a problem.' Bellos refers to her own marriage as a case in point. 'It was intended to be for life, but it lasted ten years.'

She feels that the important elements of marriage and civil partnerships are also being undermined in other respects. 'I do think that commitment is something many people want. Children do sense when their parents are unhappy though. If more thought were given to the institution of marriage, and partnerships, not the wedding dress and all the rest of it, that would be for the better. We've made marriage a commodity and in doing so devalued it.'

In relation to gay marriages, Bellos sees equality between same-sex and mixed-sex couples as having been the driving force behind the introduction of civil partnerships. 'The Human Rights Act was the impetus. It was discrimination against gay people that they couldn't have the privileges of heterosexuals. It didn't matter how long two gay men or lesbians had lived together, they couldn't benefit. It was blatantly unfair. The government was forced to legislate.'

The gay community wanted to be able to enjoy the same benefits as married couples. 'The impetus was both rights and public commitment. There were instances where the family of a deceased person rather than his partner inherited everything, all sorts of injustices. There was an absence of equality, they were treated as though their relationships didn't exist.'

Personally, Bellos has no issue with a distinction between civil partnerships and marriage. 'The government could have extended marriage to same-sex couples but they succumbed to the lobbying of the fundamentalists. For my own part, I'm delighted with a civil partnership—everyone referred to it as "getting married" and got very excited—it got bigger and bigger! Friends and family all over the world have got very into the celebrations.

Civil partnerships differ in more than name, as Bellos describes. 'The words are very similar. What is different is that you don't have to utter the words in the same way that you have to with marriage. In civil partnerships it's the act of signing which is important. Basically it's the same as a registry office wedding, just the words aren't mandatory.'

Moving on to another new area of legislation for same-sex couples, gay couples' right to adopt, Bellos is firm. 'I can't imagine why there is a problem. Anyone who adopts or fosters has to meet eligibility criteria—if only all parents had to.'

And she doesn't think that having parents of the opposite sex matters. 'What about all these men who never see their children? And what about boarding schools? And also remember that many lesbians and gay men have friends and family of the opposite sex. We forget about the extended family. The extended family provides male role models too—the men in children's lives might not always be their fathers.'

Generally Bellos sees the role of the extended family as very important. 'Children having love and stability is something I absolutely support, but it's not always possible in the real world. But love and stability and support from the community could help the isolated family problem. The thing about the extended family is that maybe it can be somewhere that gives you support that you're not getting from mummy and daddy.'

When it comes to childcare, Bellos believes in variety—and balance. 'Different childcare arrangements, engaging grandparents and the French APE[1] for example, are a good idea. I think a mixture is a good idea. There's nothing wrong with a good nursery but it goes back to making working hours shorter: long hours in childcare—for example eight hours in nursery—that is difficult.

'All babies are different. It would be wrong to be dogmatic. But I do think that breast-feeding is important, so ideally a child should be nine months to a year before it goes to nursery. Childcare is very demanding for parents, having some respite is also important. It's also good for children to get used to different settings.'

Fay Weldon
Author

Professor Fay Weldon is a novelist and Professor of Creative Writing at Brunel University.

Fay Weldon's view is that the last three decades have brought about fundamental changes in the way we view the family. 'Thirty years ago it was assumed that the purpose of marriage was procreation and the wife would be content to stay home and raise babies. Indeed, then it was possible—one man's wage being sufficient to support a family. No longer. Mothers have no choice now but to go out to work and the children suffer as a consequence. In effect, with its childcare programmes, incentives for women who earn, and the lengthening of the school day (in Germany schools close at mid-day!) the state seems prepared to take over the parental role. We are breeding kibbutz children—and that was not an experiment that worked.'

Once vociferously feminist, Weldon now sees a downside to that particular revolution. 'In the old paternalist society men had all the fun, women were oppressed, and the children got the benefit. Now women have the fun, men get the blame and the children are disadvantaged.'

Perhaps she has veered to the Right? 'It depends upon what you see as the Right. I was certainly brought up as a socialist. All the films, books, art, I was exposed to presented the far Left in a favourable light: one absorbed it with one's mother's milk. If so many of our creative artists and intellectuals are today "on the Left" it is as much to do with conditioning as rational judgment—they are what Stalin would have called "useful idiots". The worker's struggle was what it was all about: the old order had to be destroyed. Now I am not so sure. There was a lot to be said for the old order, for the old institutions. The bourgeoisie have been epatéed almost to extinction.'

Weldon sees the problem of the 'Left' as its inability to come to terms with the difference between individuals. 'In theory all children are born equally competent, but any mother can tell you that are not. Some are academic, some are not: our educational system, insisting that all are born the same, ends up blaming the teachers for failing to educate. It throws good money after bad trying to achieve the impossible. Or else blames the 'middle class' for unfairly cornering all the advantages. Yet we are educating children to become upwardly socially mobile and do better in life—in other words to join the middle classes.

'Intelligence—however we define it—has a large inheritable component; the competent and clever give birth to the competent and clever—it is not a conspiracy, just what happens. We are left with a fine old educational disaster, making the majority of children miserable sitting exams they can't possibly pass. (Even severely autistic children have to go through the motions of following the national curriculum.) The old secondary mod/grammar school divide—which provided me with my own social mobility, and a free university education—worked better: fewer children ended up humiliated or excluded.'

The denial of difference, Weldon maintains, now suffuses our society, to its detriment. 'We must all be thin non-smokers, or be stigmatised. Even the difference between men and women must be minimised. If studies demonstrate that the female menstrual period limits the efficiency of women in the workplace, or in the university, the current answer is to deny there is a problem, not attempt to remedy it. As with "the bell curve" controversy. If research says that there are more men than women at the extremities of the normal distribution curve, or that the Chinese are better at passing exams than Europeans, than West Africans, then surely the answer is to work out what we mean by "intelligence" and why some people relate to problems on paper more than others, not fly into a frenzy of total denial that any of this can be true. We should be less sensitive, more pragmatic. An observation is not necessarily a criticism.' She applies the 'denial of difference' to our treatment of faiths. 'Religion too. The argument here is that there is no difference between one religion and another. But of course there is. Christianity is a religion based on doubt: 'Dear God, I believe, help thou my unbelief'. It has fostered science and technological advance. Islam is full of certainties and against change: Hinduism and Buddhism are quietist—it being left to Karma not human effort to bring about social justice. Dawkins's atheism is in itself so passionately believed as to be a religion in itself.

'I was brought up in a society which took the New Testament as a workable basis for social justice, so naturally I will believe Christianity is "best" and female circumcision and stoning women for adultery in the name of religion is "worst"—though many in Islam will feel it is a small price to pay for a stable society in which marriages do not collapse and sex is taken seriously. I presume a lot of women feel happier and more secure when they go into the street veiled. When and if women achieve economic independence they may not feel this. But to see all religions as the same is folly. They throw us into entirely different modes of life. Again, we see the denial of difference as the nervous and fearful reaction of a political class which does not trust its own people—it has forgotten it is meant to be working towards the greatest good of the greatest number. I am a John Stuart Mill fan, if anything. Does that make me Left, or Right?'

Political correctness in general is a problem, argues Weldon. 'It is so easy for "the Left" to corner the moral high ground—how nice it would indeed be to "end poverty in Africa"—but the attempt seems to be not so much to bring about a perfect world as to demonstrate that others are in the wrong. It can be patronising and ineffective, more concerned with the feel-good factor (me good, them bad, me wear bangle to prove it), with political correctness and image, than actually achieving justice in our own society.'

To an extent the paper Weldon reads has reflected her changing views. 'The *Guardian* was once my natural choice, but I have stopped taking it. We must all think like Polly, Harriet, Cherie. It's too bad! I read the *Telegraph* for a bit until its preoccupation with murdered girls became too much, and now read the *International Herald Tribune*, because it actually contains some news.'

Like the *Guardian*, feminism has been middle-class-centric, says Weldon. 'Of course the feminist revolution was a good thing. But its critics were right in some of their arguments. It was indeed a middle-class movement. All women were to have satisfying "careers"—and there was little acknowledgement that some women would rather stay home and look after the kids and be supported by a man: that employment could be a chore rather than a pleasure and a right. Today's working woman seldom has as many children as she would like. She doesn't have the time, the money or the energy. Today's family man with a working wife is deprived of the paternalistic pleasures of "looking after" either wife or children. And the children look to their teachers to provide the socialisation that once the parents did. Patterns of living have changed: not always for the best.'

Weldon moves on to non-resident fathers and the Child Support Agency. 'The State's attempt to bring back fatherhood—or at any rate make fathers pay. It's an uphill battle: of course it keeps going wrong. The instinctive reaction of today's man in that if the child is not under his roof, and the wife not in the bed, he can hardly be expected to pay. What for? An hour or so of passion, her responsibility as much as his? Before the Eighties, before women had control of contraception, and it was up to the man to take responsibility, the thinking was he "made her pregnant". So he paid. Now the man's thinking is "she gets pregnant..." so he won't pay. She didn't get an abortion when she could have, and the law gives her the house, what more does she want? She's not going to get it from me!'

Weldon's views on whether parental separation per se is a problem are mixed. 'It depends. Some people do it easily: both the marriage and the divorce are little more than the opportunity for a party. For some it the source of great distress. If there aren't children it hardly matters anyway: if there are children there's denial in the personal sphere. "I've forgotten him," says the mother, "the bastard! My child must forget too."But the child does not. "I'm going to marry again," says the father. "Lucky child, now she'll have two homes, two mothers!" But the child doesn't feel in the least lucky. Nor does the child feel lucky whose mother, feeling the urge to fulfil herself, decides to give birth without the benefit of a live-in father. It would be very convenient if it were so, but it seldom is.

'The mother-father-child relationship is complicated at the best of times: multiple mothers and fathers make matters worse. Of course too many of our children are depressed, won't learn, can't learn, take to drugs and drink, look mean and knowing before their time: become teenage mothers and fathers themselves. At least then there's someone around to love.'

Marriage is something Weldon definitely sees as unequivocally relevant today. 'Of course, though more and more of us seem fated to live alone. We have trouble getting together, pairing off. We fear loneliness, rightly. We fear old age. The young fear "commitment", confusing it with boredom. Therapists dismiss "love" as neurotic dependency, but in the end most of us want to be in some kind of permanent relationship—if only we can find the right person. Most of us in the end do. The marriage rate is going up—the pendulum may be beginning to swing back the other way. There is cause for hope.'

There is less hope that men and women will ever be wholly equal in their involvement with children. 'Mothers, through breast-feeding, have a sensuous relationship with their children that is hard for the father to emulate. Nature will have its way: she is all soft and custom built for mothering: he is all bony, whatever his principles. The price of gender equality, as today's young mother tries to socialise the male into doing his fair share of parenting, is eternal vigilance, and sometimes the price is too high for a woman to pay. And there are noble exceptions—some men make better mothers than women ever do. Sometimes fathers bond and mothers don't. To insist on our rights can be counterproductive. Difference, when it comes to child rearing, is not to be denied. We could just all try for a fair division of labour.'

Weldon is not keen on the idea of the government championing particular family outcomes. 'It is not really the business of governments to condone, or otherwise, the way people live or don't live. It is a dangerous business: supposing they get it wrong? This government seems to have done so. Labour, for example, wanted the old traditional family structure to break down—on apparently ideological grounds—and altered tax structures to hasten the demise of the old ways. It encouraged—indeed bullied—young mothers to go out to work, gave support and housing to single mothers so having babies became a desirable "life choice", and with the new civil marriages made it clear that marriage has nothing to do with procreation. A wedding now means a party, and that's about all. But all these steps towards a less formal structure of society, in which we are all loose cannons bumping into each other, moved by the transient emotions of the day, freed from the "backward" institutions of the past—Sunday morning now means the shopping mall, not Church—seemed to produce a yet unhappier population—if one looks at levels of crime, mental illness, vandalism, falling literacy and indeed birth-rate of the indigenous population. Life itself becomes something you don't necessarily want to pass on—and if you do, how can you afford to? You don't have the time, energy or housing for a baby. Let alone a permanent partner. It has been an experiment that failed—and the fact that it was an experiment has never been put to the electorate.'

Instead, Weldon wishes the government would stick to informing citizens. 'How nice it would be if government would restrict itself to giving information about what suits its citizens statistically—i.e. let it be known that children in nursery schools suffer, that children without fathers do worse than children who have them around, that younger women have healthier children, that partnerships break up—what is the figure?—four times as fast?—as marriages and so on. Then it is up to the citizen to decide whether to take any notice or not, not for a government to take the moral lead. Let it stick to the business of defending the realm, building schools and hospitals, and giving ten per cent of the joint wealth to the hapless poor, as the religions of most cultures suggest.'

Jo Elvin
Editor of *Glamour* magazine

Jo Elvin is editor of Glamour *magazine. Elvin launched the UK edition of* Glamour *in 2001, and it has since become Britain's biggest-selling women's magazine. In 2004 the* Observer *named Elvin one of the 80 young people who would 'define the country's culture, politics and economics for a generation'.*

Jo Elvin sees *Glamour's* success as lying in its accessibility and breadth. '*Glamour* magazine is aimed at what we call the "premium economy" flier: readers with a very *Vogue* outlook, but who don't necessarily have the disposable income. Everybody feels that there is something in it for them. It's accessible for lower-income-end readers but also higher-end readers don't feel scuzzy reading it. *Glamour* is a very good, all-around package incorporating fashion, celebrities, love and relationships and politics. When it was launched it was something new for the UK, it filled a void.'

Glamour is the most popular women's magazine in Britain and Elvin therefore considers the *Glamour* reader to be representative of young women in the UK. 'Basically it's always sold so well. There wasn't anything so shamelessly mass-market before.' Elvin also stays very much in touch with her readers. 'We do surveys a couple of times a year but it's via readers' emails that we really keep in touch. But you can't edit prescriptively, you need to edit instinctively. If the team and I are interested in something, for example, our readers generally are. Many feature ideas come from conversations with our friends in the wine bar.'

Celebrities are a central part of each *Glamour* issue. But, Elvin argues, readers know where to delineate between their lives and those of celebrities—the recent spate of celebrity adoptions being a case in point. 'I think readers are interested because Madonna is adopting, but that they wouldn't be going out and buying a Namibian child themselves. Our readers are not ready to have children, but they love the gossip.'

On the subject of children, Elvin finds that fertility issues, rather than babies, are of greater interest to the *Glamour* reader. 'We don't really run any stories about children or parenting, but sometimes we run stories about things like reproductive health. In our forthcoming issue there is an article about younger women counting backwards, about where they would like to be lifestyle-wise in several years and panicking about how to get there. This is a big topic at the moment. The media, particularly the *Daily Mail*, loves an "egg panic".'

Elvin does think that readers have aspirations about children for the future which are fairly universal. 'Most women have fairytale values about being able to have everything. I myself have a young daughter and you just don't realise until you've done it how hard it is to have it all. A lot of women are deferring priorities like children. They don't want to be in a position where they can't afford their mortgage—and if they wait they'll be in a stronger financial position.'

Glamour readers probably want both career and children rather than to become homemakers, Elvin would guess. 'I think it's more likely that women with it all idealise now about the perfect balance.' Going part-time is one way of doing this, yet Elvin recognises its difficulties. 'As an employer this is frustrating as the most experienced don't want to work full-time.'

Part-time fathers on the other hand, are a rarity Elvin notes. 'Stay-at-home dads are still a dot rather than a blob on the landscape.' The workplace, she feels is partly to blame. 'Flexibility to accommodate childcare is not really a concept in employers' minds. Couples personally come to arrangements. But even in good partnerships, the bulk of childcare responsibility tends to fall on the woman.'

For readers 'who are likely to be without children' however, this inequality is not yet a concern. 'They are too busy worrying about their bodies and bank balances.' Yet, readers are '…probably living with a partner', so relationships are an important topic. 'How to keep the spark alive in their relationships is a major issue. For many readers who had lived with their partners for three or four years it is "make-or-break" time. We do a lot of features about "where do I go from here relationship-wise?" This period of readers' lives is a real milestone for many women—we once even featured an article about the "quarter-life crisis".'

Ultimately Elvin believes that *Glamour* readers—and young women generally—want something similar in life: to marry. 'Most people are very traditional and want to get married. Even if people don't want the wedding and the dress, they want the partner for life.'

Marie O'Riordan
Editor of Marie Claire

Editor of Marie Claire *since April 2001, Marie O'Riordan is a frequent spokeswoman for Marie Stopes International and female-related organisations and charities.*

One of the things which distinguishes *Marie Claire* is its often thought-provoking features, such as a recent article on domestic violence around the world. 'We call it our "global perspective"; it's our unique selling point,' says *Marie Claire* editor Marie O'Riordan. 'I wasn't the first editor, but before my time, in its early days, the magazine was up against *Vogue* and *Elle* in the market. We used to describe *Marie Claire* as the glossy with a brain—the difference is that it is fashion with something to read. With these reads often touching on serious issues. Other magazines didn't have fashion as well as investigative journalism. The only magazine with reading material in it was really *Cosmopolitan* but the content was sexual, endless advice on how to please your man.'

O'Riordan describes the *Marie Claire* reader. 'She's a median age of about 30, she's a professional—the assumption is that she has been through tertiary education and that she's interested in a career, not just a job.'

When it comes to readers' personal profiles, *Marie Claire* makes a point of not pigeonholing, O'Riordan explains. 'We edit the magazine from the perspective that we work very hard not to classify the reader by her marital status and the state of her reproductive system. A lot of the other magazines define their readers: *Red's* for mums, *Cosmopolitan's* for singles interested in sex... *Marie Claire* very proudly chooses not to define readers like this—what distinguishes the *Marie Claire* reader is her urbane attitude. We take it for read that you have a healthy sex life and family life. We try to cover the family-related issues in the context of women's changing role within society: for example, features on surviving divorce, step-parenting roles, that sort of thing.'

Work/life balance, O'Riordan argues, features strongly both in women's lives and the magazine. 'It's a huge issue for women in Britain and we try to reflect this through features to do with female leadership, for example, or managing family life or sexism in the workplace. I was looking at a survey recently which showed that women were dropping out of FTSE 100 companies and setting up businesses themselves. Internet business is also a real liberation for women, as it allows them to work from home — and today we've seen in the news that women are the biggest single group using the Internet: for community purposes, for swapping information.'

In line with an interest in work/life balance is *Marie Claire*'s hope for gender equality between parents. 'We edit with the assumption that the man is equally enlightened. We know this isn't the reality, but it's the aspiration. In an ideal society paternity leave would be equal to maternity leave and men would be equally involved in childcare. That's the ideal that we're aiming for.'

O'Riordan does think that men are now becoming more involved in childcare. 'That's definitely happening—at least for educated women, their partners are becoming more switched-on. Their partners are saying "this is a partnership". But society isn't completely in tune with this; it's very unusual for a man to reduce his hours and work part-time, for example.'

She sees some industries as being more parenting-friendly than others. 'The creative industries can be more accommodating because of project work. But not all of them. I often have lunch with managers in the fashion industry and their maternity policies aren't as extensive as our own in magazine journalism. Certainly outside these industries, though, particularly for lower-class women, going part-time is likely to be even more difficult.'

O'Riordan doesn't think that more women in an industry will necessarily mean a culture of greater flexibility. 'Women in management positions are not always willing to help other women. They feel that they have got where they have the hard way, and they don't want to draw attention to themselves as being different from men. Plus, right at the top of the power structure, it's still mostly men running the show. Basically employers are reluctant to facilitate parenting because it's an expense that drops straight off the bottom line. In terms of facilitating parenting in employment we are more like America—though better—and less like, say, northern Europe, which seems to have more progressive maternity policies.'

Marie Claire readers want a balance rather than an either/or situation when it comes to work and children, O'Riordan argues. 'Opting out of the workplace isn't seen as the ideal thing to do, and it's quite rare among our readers. Because our constituency is largely middle-class, they are lucky to be able to afford to leave the workforce in the first place. But when they do, they may feel ousted by their female contemporaries—it's not a wholly comfortable experience. Women who do opt out can lose their confidence quite easily, and their friendships can become strained. But I couldn't say that there is a blanket scenario—if you are the person going to work, for example, you might envy the person who is staying at home. We ran a feature about this called "The Mummy Wars".'

What is clear, however, is that young women's aspirations are less utopian today. 'I think that having it all was an '80s slogan. Now compromise is actually OK, a three-day week is OK. You're probably not going to make it to senior management levels but it's satisfactory. But I don't feel that we can even achieve that very easily now: if that was achievable we could be happy with that.'

O'Riordan sees class as essential to the discussion. 'I always feel that the magazine—and a lot of the media generally—is the voice of the middle classes. The discussion of whether to go part-time or not is a luxury. It's not on the cards for a lot of women, there's no discussion about it. It's the luxury of the middle classes.'

Moving on to the subject of marriage, O'Riordan sees it as having evolved with changes to women's lives. 'There's a certain romance associated with marriage for our readers. I think that women feel less trapped than before: if a relationship fails, there is more incentive to get out. And opportunity to do so. I think through economic independence and through education, women can afford to feel more empowered. In this respect, I think that relationship break-ups are a signal of a more privileged generation of women.

'Weddings are still an enormous source of business. Marriage is still the dream, falling in love and being monogamous and staying together forever. The family unit is still very much the ideal.'

O'Riordan refers to a survey recently commissioned by *Marie Claire*. 'The survey shows that for 96 per cent of women friendship is still the most important thing with a partner. The vast majority of women want a partner for life. There is evidence of sexual freedom, and evidence of people having sexual partnerships without wanting it to go any further than sex. But people still want the same things. The ideals, the aspirations, are everything that women have always wanted. They're holding out for a lifetime partner, with experimentation before they commit. This experimentation is progressive and relates to increased privileges. Marriage often comes after children nowadays—and to juggle work and children you need a committed partner.'

O'Riordan feels that not every bit of change to relationships is positive however. 'The flip side is that there is less tolerance about making things work. The current generation are strong enough but it's arguable that they don't try hard enough. But my belief is that people don't walk away lightly from relationships. Even though divorce is easier it's never truly problem-free: everybody involved is traumatised by relationship breakdown.'

Deborah Joseph
Editor of Brides Magazine

Deborah Joseph is editor of Brides Magazine, *a wedding magazine from the publishers of* Vogue.

Brides Magazine is the best-selling bridal magazine in both the UK and the US, something editor Deborah Joseph attributes to its unique recipe. 'It's the most fashionable but without being edgy.' With weddings apparently still associated with tradition, 'edginess' isn't desirable – as a competing magazine recently discovered: '*Wedding Day*, another bridal magazine, has just folded because it was too fashiony when what people want is traditional.'

Joseph sees marriage as having made a comeback of sorts. 'Marriage has become cool again. All my friends, whatever their political persuasions—even the most Left-wing "hippy" ones—are either married now or want to get married. Marriage is in fashion at the moment: the "ladette" culture is over now and people like Zoë Ball and Gwyneth Paltrow have all got married.'

But ultimately she thinks that there is more than fashion behind why people want to marry today. 'I think that the number one reason for getting married is commitment—being willing to commit in front of people says something about your relationship—and the second, social status. I think that the social status part is especially important for women: when women have a ring on their finger they are viewed as more of an adult.' The social pressure is something Joseph thinks is also strong. 'People who aren't married panic after a certain age, I think.'

Financial security, however, Joseph sees as less of a draw today. 'Women don't necessarily get married for security reasons now—you can see that from the way that many women now marry younger men. And even when women marry wealthy men they often keep working.'

As a result, Joseph believes that negatives such as chauvinism have become disassociated with marriage. 'You can be a feminist within marriage. Women don't change their name anymore, men share household duties and many men are now great cooks.'

Joseph thinks that generally a lot has changed in relation to the roles between men and women in the home, and that this was making for far more equal partnerships. 'Male chefs such as Jamie Oliver have really made cooking acceptable for men. Cleaners have become an everyday phenomenon. This means that women are not stuck doing a full day's work and then having to do another full day's work by cleaning the house and having to cook the dinner. There's also more flexibility in the workforce, which makes marriage and children more compatible with a career.'

The wedding itself is certainly something Joseph believes has a lot to do with marriage's popularity today—as well as the later marrying age. 'People are getting married later because of the cost of getting married. In the olden days parents used to pay for the wedding, but now couples wait until they are financially independent. One of my friends recently said that they couldn't yet afford the wedding they had in mind, that they wanted. I told them just to get on with it anyway. But that's not what they wanted, they wanted to wait until they could have the wedding of their dreams.'

"Dream" weddings generally mean expensive ones and Joseph thinks that the popular media have influenced people's aspirations a great deal. 'The *OK* and *Hello* [magazines] phenomenon has had a big impact on couples' wedding ceremonies.'

But definitely the most significant influence has been the 'Jordan effect'. 'At the moment marriage is trendy: Jordan's wedding has had a huge influence, the whole fairytale thing. Women are getting to live out their dreams through their weddings.' (Glamour model Jordan married singer Peter Andre in a Disneyesque ceremony involving a pink wedding gown with a seven-yard train and a Cinderella-style horse and carriage.)

Joseph points out that the wedding industry is keen to oblige celebrity inspiration. 'Many wedding dress designers are now also making high street versions of their wedding designs.'

The wedding does seem to be very much about the bride. 'The whole wedding and all the preparation is definitely a very female thing, men don't really get involved. This is probably because they've not grown up their whole lives playing with dolls and pretending to get married.' When it comes to the financial side, however, men are very involved. 'Couples do share the *cost* of the weddings, though. They save up for the wedding together, often using shared bank accounts particularly when they've been living together beforehand.'

With the sums at stake, the average investment from both bride and groom is enormous. 'We're just waiting for new figures on the cost of weddings, but it's thought that it's going to be about £20,000 now. The average cost of the wedding dress was £800, but again it's thought that this figure has now risen to about £1,000. The bodice style dress is the most popular,' she adds, 'for the simple reason that it's the most flattering.'

That some couples now borrow to pay for their weddings isn't surprising in light of these sorts of figures. 'Some couples get into debt to pay for their weddings. But the thing is that couples would prefer to have the day of their dreams, and pay it off over a lifetime, than scrimp.' She doesn't think we need be too concerned though. 'A lot of people live on credit now, it's the way we live: cars, holidays, houses, all on credit.'

Joseph sees weddings as having become both more important today and more personalised. 'Individuality and a unique twist are becoming more important to the bride who is keen for her wedding day to reflect her personality. So a couple might choose a venue which reflects their interests. For example, if they like scuba diving they might get married underwater or if they like travelling they might get married abroad.'

It's not just women who love weddings, Joseph points out. 'Weddings always make the front pages—newspapers are obsessed with marriage. It's probably because amongst all the depressing news marriages are something happy to celebrate. After 9/11 there was a massive upsurge of marriages of people who hadn't walked up the aisle and now wanted to.'

Marriages that don't go to plan are also front-page favourites. 'There is a newish phenomenon,' Joseph comments on the rising divorce rates, 'called "starter marriages" where couples get married in their twenties and then divorced in their thirties.'

She sees women's financial independence as an explanation for the proliferation in divorce today. 'Women are more financially independent now. Whereas years ago they had to stick around, like their mothers had to, today they are financially able to leave an unhappy marriage. It's the same for older women too. Couples are increasingly getting divorced in their fifties. As people live longer, older couples are thinking: we're going to live another 50 years, do we really want to be stuck together that long?'

Another explanation might be pre-marital cohabitation, she suggests. 'I heard somewhere that research said if you cohabited for one year there was more chance of success in your marriage, whereas cohabiting for longer has a negative effect. Maybe cohabiting dilutes it? Perhaps you lose that something special. Or maybe,' she adds, 'you don't get that psychological shift if you've lived together.'

Deidre Sanders
The *Sun's* problem page editor

Deidre Sanders has been the Sun's *agony aunt—'Dear Deidre'—for more than 25 years. She has counselling training and has just finished a six-year-spell as a trustee of the Family and Parenting Institute.*

When it comes to family-related issues, Deidre Sanders says that troubled partnerships top the list of *Sun* readers' worries. 'It's got to be to do with relationship breakdown, when the parents' relationship is under some pressure, perhaps there's been an infidelity or there's drug or alcohol addiction, or getting into debt and financial worries.'

Sanders feels that these sorts of strains on the adults in the family can often have negative effects on the children. 'When the parents in a family are stressed they are often not able to put the energy into their children, and very quickly you've got a very unhappy family.' Extended family, she thinks, can take some of the pressure off parents but we should be careful not to make too many assumptions. 'There's a real danger that we generalise about the family and assume they're all wonderful and supportive. In fact the extended family can be a very mixed blessing, a lot of pressures can actually come from the parents and grandparents. This really is a time of such change. We think all grandparents are cuddly but some can be demanding and very critical.'

How best to support families more generally is also a complex issue, she says. 'People from some backgrounds find it easier to reach out, for example. The middle classes seem to find it easier to get support. My daughter, for instance, has a six-month old baby and has moved to the other end of the country. Although she knew nobody there, she's fine and making friends easily because she's mobile, she's got the confidence and she's articulate. But if you're not articulate and not mobile and it's not in the culture, it's much more difficult to reach out for help.'

Sanders sees that this is an issue with some of her readers. 'We get a lot of letters which say, "we can't go out because we have no family near us". What saddens me is that many people do not feel able to draw on their friends, which I did a lot when I had young children. Not having other people to help out makes it very hard and makes families feel very isolated.'

For this reason Sanders thinks single parents need more support—but that we need to be sensitive about offering it. 'Single parents get very touchy if you suggest they are struggling. But it's very lonely often, especially as many people are not used to the idea of inviting people round for a cup of coffee, and of course single parents are even more isolated than parents with a partner sharing the role in the family.'

Support in the form of some of the government schemes which have been criticised as 'nanny-stateish', Sanders sees as actually very valuable. 'Parenting classes are great—if anything they haven't got enough of them! My big plea, and I'm really banging on about them, is health visitors—increase their funding at the local level. I also want to see more easily accessible parenting classes everywhere—with good childcare facilities, of course! The National Academy for Parenting Practitioners should help but an awful lot will depend on what happens to funding on the ground. There are an awful lot of ante-natal classes but precious little on parenting once you've actually had the baby. All they bang on about is breast-feeding, which is important but not the only thing.'

Sanders argues that health visitors once played a very valuable role. 'The way it used to be was that first the midwife used to come and then the health visitor. One of the best things was that families weren't labelled as problem families as everyone had a health visitor, it was totally non-stigmatising. The health visitor would see how things were shaping up and then if there appeared to be problems would come back.

'The other great thing about health visitors was that they could get the mum into a mother and toddler group, for example, or would know that ten doors down there was another mum in a similar situation. The problem now is that the health visitor says "we won't come back unless you ring us", so that people actually need to reach out, which can be hard when you're bogged down with post-natal depression.'

Yet although Sanders can see that parents are under many pressures today, in some respects she feels that they do not go into parenting with enough realism. 'Something which strikes me as so odd is the way that people seem to be unwilling to accept the idea that some income might be lost when you have children. Yes you do lose income, obviously, someone's got to put the time into children.' Sanders points out that children don't just cost today, they demand too. 'The whole pressure of consumerism is a very real issue. I can see how this has changed looking at my own daughters' friends: one is 19 and the other 30 and there's been a real change in atmosphere among young people even between these two ages. One of the problems seems to be that everybody now feels entitled to a celebrity lifestyle. This can be really hard for those of us who are only ever going to achieve the norm, leaving people feeling very hard done by and disillusioned. I think previously people accepted a hum-drum level of life was normal.'

Sanders sees another newer pressure on children as being the fact that often both parents work long hours today. 'Both parents saying goodbye to their kids at seven o'clock in the morning and then picking them up again at seven p.m. isn't great for the children. I don't believe in "quality time"; by and large children want "boring" time. I passed up career opportunities to be there more for my children. Having said that, the pressures are much fiercer now: it's all very well saying you would like to be at home, but what if that means not being able to pay the mortgage?'

Money has also got very caught up in marriage, Sanders says. 'What I regret is that the average cost of a wedding now is about £13,000. I wish I could unhook weddings from Jordan-esque, celebrity-style extravagance—it's back to that idea of everyone wanting the celebrity life-style—and have simple weddings. There didn't used to be all this extravagance. There were society weddings of course but many people got married simply at the church or register office and had a cup of tea or drink in the pub afterwards.'

Sanders sees this consumerist emphasis overtaking the point of marriage. 'Marriage should be about commitment to the relationship. Now I hear from people who aren't getting married just because they can't afford a big do. People are putting off making a commitment because of that. It's putting the cart before the horse, it's barmy.'

Whatever the meaning of marriage, however, Sanders doesn't believe that it should be tied up in policy. 'I'm really cross about all this Conservative marriage stuff. How people choose to live their personal relationships is private, it's not the state's concern. And I object to the idea of tax-breaks for married couples because I think that they just constrain choice. It's very easy to distort the figures that are used to promote the case for marriage and it's not about frog-marching couples down to the register office.

'Yes, married couples tend to have more stable relationships, and that is good for children, but it's not the piece of paper itself that makes the difference. It's that the sort of people who choose and feel able to afford to get married these days are the sort of people who are going to have more stable relationships anyway. I do see it as the government's business to help families raise happy, balanced children who will grow up into adults able to make a positive contribution to society, but it's not easily achieved just by making their parents marry. What we have to do is educate young people about relationships, both their own and those within families, to help them understand what an enormous responsibility it is to bring a child into the world.

'I still receive dismaying problems from teens who opt for parenting as a way to get an adult identity. We really need to address the issues of those teens who live in a dead-end area, who are truanting, who are not doing so well at school. How do we help them feel they belong to society instead of prowling the perimeters, help them see a way through to a constructive future?'

Many of today's strategies she considers to be unsuitable. 'The whole ASBO mentality, exclusion orders, demonising children—I hate all of it, we need to address the underlying causes. My dad was a head teacher and when there were problems with a pupil he would go round to their house and talk to the parents: schools were a strong community and difficult children weren't just excluded and given up on, but of course my father could rely on most parents being open to his suggestions, working with him not against him.'

These positives are something some schools are struggling to foster, Sanders worries. 'School is children's first example of the outside world and if it doesn't impress them then it can have a very negative impact. If children come from a background which is chaotic, schools should be an oasis of continuity and stability. Some manage this brilliantly, some sadly do not.'

Whilst Sanders would like to see much more easily available adult counselling, she feels the even more urgent demand today is for support for young people, in and out of school. 'Relationship advice and counselling is not a panacea, but Relate's work with separating parents and the work that it is doing in schools get very impressive results. One of my team is a "Talk-time" counsellor in a school and gives us very positive feedback. I would like to see help like that in every school. Children suffer terribly from things going on at home and are often so powerless. Having someone to talk to is very important, and the right help at the right time can turn a child's life around.'

Virginia Ironside
The Independent's *problem page editor*

An author and journalist, Virginia Ironside has been an agony aunt for the last 30 years and currently edits the 'Dilemmas' page for the Independent.

'People want advice in a different way nowadays. They want it from more than one person,' says Virginia Ironside, problem page editor for the *Independent*. 'The attitude to advice is now more democratic: in the past there were those who knew and those who didn't. It was much more of a leader and led thing. That has changed I think, especially with the arrival of the internet. Now there is a range of options for people to turn to for advice: friends, the internet, their doctor... and they mix it all up into a big soup. It's now a case of ask the experts *and* your mum and your friends... There's also less shame in asking for advice today. This seems to be a social trend.'

Although no particular question comes up the most, Ironside has noticed some concerns coming to the fore. 'The problem of loneliness and living alone is a primary concern, particularly among young men. The number of young men who don't know what their role is now — "new men". They seem to be less able to move out of home, they spend time on computers at home rather than in an office and they are getting isolated.'

Ironside points to an ostensible positive which can also be problematic. 'There is so much choice, it is a tremendous stress. There's nothing like choice to give you a nervous breakdown. It's not just big decisions like when to have children, even going to the supermarket for children is stressful: even which fish-fingers or sausages? As you don't have to worry about having enough to eat, you worry about *what* to eat. All sorts of things like E-numbers and gluten have become worrying in a world of choice.'

Ironside also sees parental separation as highly problematic for children. 'It is not usually very happy for the children when parents split up. On the whole I think children would like their parents to stay together until they leave home. It is difficult enough growing up; to have a couple of stable figures, who you are relying on to be there, who then crumble, is not good.

'I think it's best to try to stick together. I am ashamed of myself for not having managed to, in that I split up with my son's father when he was only 18 months. I'm rather po-faced about that side of things. And I have to say, even though it is not fashionable, I am not keen on single-parent side effects if it can possibly be avoided.' Ironside doesn't consider class to be relevant to parental separation. 'I think it's a class-free thing affecting everyone.'

She regards grandparents as a vital resource, and Ironside loves being one herself. 'Grandparents are not of so great importance now and that is a pity. Grandparents are like a House of Lords, a European Court of Appeal that children can turn to. One of the reasons that grandparents don't play such a great role any more is because they don't want to. I see it with friends of mine: "You think we're going to baby-sit? We're not baby-sitting, we're going to the Bahamas".'

Ironside sees issues with combining work and childcare. 'It's very difficult for me to say—my mother worked and I certainly wasn't happy. I didn't think it was a good thing. If you're going to have children, look after them. Childcare normally takes up one salary anyway so one parent at home would be a good situation. Childcare needs to be consistent: a new au pair every year, for example, doesn't make for this consistency.

'I'm not mad about the government encouraging mothers to go to work. I still find that whole economic thing—paying someone to look after your child, difficult. I wonder how beneficial it is for everyone involved: I'm not sure mothers get that much out of the arrangement. Obviously a depressed stay-at-home parent isn't a good thing either. I think the situation must be somewhere in between. It is very difficult to generalise though, a lot is down to the individual and individual circumstance.'

She thinks that men are more involved in childcare, but that there hasn't been a revolution. 'I think it's changing a little but not as much as people think. Although there might be some change among the young men in North London and Brixton, I don't think that's the case generally. I suspect there has not been very much change.

'It's the beginning of a slow revolution. It is a sort of luxury, an affluence thing. For things to change would mean a huge shift in working patterns.'

Love, Ironside argues, is at the centre of good parenting. 'A mixture of intelligence and love. A child must feel love, and loved above all, not just loved. If a child has this love then all other things fall into place. We all need to know that somebody cares for us more than anything. We all fall short of it but that is the aim.'

Structure in a child's life is also very important she says. 'Boundaries and structures are very important; sitting round the table—or all around the telly at the same time, life generally not being chaotic. Rearing children is like planting seeds, they need the same consistent care.'

When it comes to government initiatives like parenting classes, Ironside is luke-warm. 'I can't see anything wrong with them. When I was bringing up my children I'd have been bloody grateful to get good advice if I was having a problem. Advice generally I think is welcome; probably a bit of advice can be as good as a tenner—although sometimes a tenner is better. But money isn't always the solution; look at very poor countries where some children are brought up very well.'

Ironside thinks that it is legitimate to talk about ideal parenting structures. 'Of course: two people to be there for you. And it doesn't matter what sex they are. Two parents mean two courts of appeal as opposed to one. Two's better than one, simple as that.'

Ironside believes that the government could do more to elevate the status of parenting. 'I don't know enough about it and about what other governments have done. And there are so many initiatives and so many promises that it is difficult to keep track. But they should make education more of a priority, with teachers paid as much as GPs. Bringing up children is the most important thing. That is the only important thing, making children happy and stable.'

Marriage is something which Ironside sees as useful to families. 'It is still important. My son had a girlfriend, they didn't live together, she got pregnant, he moved in, and now they're getting married. Marriage seems to be about commitment. I'm a real 1960s "marriage-is-only-a piece-of-paper" person so I was surprised by my reaction. I think that marriage is important to everyone else in the family. I suddenly feel that my daughter-in-law, like me, is getting committed to a family—there is a tying and a closening.'

Libby Brooks
Author and journalist

Former Women's Editor of the Guardian, *Libby Brooks is author of* The Story of Childhood: Growing up in Modern Britain.

Libby Brooks's assessment of recent changes in family life is mixed. 'A positive is that people are no longer staying in relationships which they are unhappy in. A negative aspect is that people seem to be putting less effort into making their relationships work. The modern "individualism" and instant gratification have propelled the minimisation of effort put into relationships.'

This picture doesn't necessarily sit well with Brooks' prerequisites for happy children. 'The common things that children want are stability, and proper boundaries. The question is how these can be enforced?'

Faced with such questions, Brooks thinks the New Labour government has to an extent struggled. 'I think that there is a political problem with the family, in that the Left feels unable to advocate anything but diversity. The Labour Party's difficulty is that they are so shy of coming out and owning that territory. They have also been very clumsy on family policy. For example, John Hutton saying a couple of days before the Labour Party conference that two parents were better than one—well we know that! They need to be a little braver.'

Nevertheless Brooks sees a resistance to too much discussion on family structure as wise. 'There is definitely a role for social policy: to make it easier to work and look after children. What the government *shouldn't* be doing is presenting a particular model of the family to adhere to. This makes everyone feel uncomfortable. The government's role is to facilitate real choice not just nominal choice.'

With these priorities in mind, Brooks thinks that the Labour Party's record on family is impressive. 'This government has done a lot to help children and families, through tax credits and Sure Start, for example.'

It is possible to make generalisations about optimal family structures, Brooks believes, without being prescriptive. 'In an ideal world there would be very serious commitment between parents—but parents don't need to be married to be good parents. And I think that a man and a woman are the optimum parenting structure because they bring different archetypes to the child's life. However this is not always possible.'

Although marriage might theoretically signal commitment, Brooks feels that the growing emphasis on the superficial elements are a distraction. 'Marriage is increasingly commercialised and about expenditure. Wedding ceremonies etc. mean that we are in danger of mythologizing marriage. In France they've introduced civil partnerships for heterosexual couples and the take-up has sky-rocketed. This suggests that the interest is in partnership rather than the weddings. The commitment in this case seems to be more of a practical one.'

Nevertheless, Brooks sees marriage as still relevant today. 'There seems to be a pro-marriage movement again. Perhaps because marriage is one of the last remaining structures we have in a world of transition and impermanence.'

Kate Bell
Head of Policy, One Parent Families/Gingerbread

Kate Bell is Head of Policy and Research at the single-parent support organisation One Parent Families/Gingerbread.

Kate Bell is keen to dispel the myths around single parenting. 'The interesting thing here in the UK is that the big increase in lone parenthood can be attributed to the rise in the 1970s and 1980s. The reason for the growth in lone-parent rates was much less to do with changes in social norms—though this had some relevance—and much more to do with economic factors, such as high unemployment, families running into debt, houses being reclaimed and the strains that these put on family life. So in other words an increase in lone parenting was much less to do with family *formation* and much more to do with families breaking up.'

In short, Bell's point is that single parents do not have a different set of values when it comes to family. 'It's not a lifestyle choice, people do not deliberately set out to become lone parents. In most cases lone parenthood is down to relationship breakdown. Also, lone parenthood is a transitory state: the average length of lone parenthood is only five years. So the whole "Little Britain" image of lone parenthood and of total value change is just inaccurate. One Parent Families/Gingerbread has been around since 1918—lone parenthood is not a new phenomenon.'

Bell is also keen to dispel misconceptions about the purpose of One Parent Families/Gingerbread. 'Sometimes One Parent Families/Gingerbread is accused of promoting lone parenthood, but we're not at all about promoting it: we see it as a period in people's lives when they need support. Their ideals aren't different, their ideal is that "I bring up my kids in a loving partnership".'

Although she regards class as relevant, Bell doesn't see single parenting as the domain only of the poor. 'I don't think it's a class issue, because we know that lone parenthood happens across the spectrum. There are all sorts of examples of people from different classes who find themselves parenting alone. However certain factors give you a better predictor of the likelihood of becoming a lone-parent family. For example, coming from a broken home and when people marry very early. So there are predictors, but it's difficult to say from one class to another.'

Comparisons across countries are also difficult to make she argues. 'The first thing to say is that it is very difficult to make a cross-country comparison. This is not just a way to fob you off with statistics, but the amount of time spent as a lone parent varies considerably from country to country. In the UK, for example, there may be a very high rate of lone parenthood at any one time, but children are spending only a short period of time in lone-parent families. Or there is a big contrast, for example, between the US and Sweden. They have very different circumstances to each other, but they both have very high rates of lone parenthood. In Sweden there are high levels of benefits and lone parents are not poor, whereas in the US there is a lot of poverty associated with lone parenthood.

'In Scandinavia lone parenthood doesn't go together with poverty: in the Unicef report[1] the Scandinavian countries did very well on children's well-being, yet they have very high rates of lone parenthood.'

Bell sees hurdles to earning an income as hampering the lives of single-parent families in the UK. 'Lone parents here face fundamental difficulties. There have been huge improvements in childcare, but many still can't afford childcare that they can trust and many cannot find flexible work. Many lone parents are on a low income—about half of all lone-parent children live below the poverty line. There have been improvements though: the number of lone-parent families living below the poverty line was 62 per cent, but there are still issues about the type of work available. Two-parent families need flexibility—one-parent families need it in spades.'

Bell feels that New Labour has made a difference to the lives of single parents, but that there is still a long way to go. 'Things which have improved are access to employment: 45 per cent of lone parents were in employment and now 56 per cent are. But this still falls short of the level of lone-parent employment in other countries and is well below lone parents' aspirations—most of whom want to be able to combine paid work with caring for their family.

'There is much more to do now: flexibility in work, particularly, is needed. The second improvement is in childcare. Extended schools, after-school clubs and children's centres are particularly important to lone parents. Thirdly, the use of tax credits. For all the bad publicity around tax credits, they have transformed the lives of many lone-parent families.'

Helping single parents combine work and childcare is crucial, Bell argues. 'It's much more complicated than lone parents not wanting to go into work. One of the founding objectives of One Parent Families when it was established in 1918 was to enable lone parents to work, and it has been outstandingly successful. We are involved with Marks and Spencer's and ASDA, for example, on programmes to help lone parents into work.'

However Bell is against the government's suggestion of forcing single parents to work once their child reaches 12 years old as of next year, and from 2010, when their youngest child reaches seven. 'The government has suggested that lone parents should shift to job-seekers allowance and be available for work. One Parent Families/Gingerbread disagrees with this approach. I don't think it will work. Lone parents need support and encouragement, not threats and sanctions. So firstly I don't think it will work and secondly I don't think Job Centre Plus has got the resources to find suitable jobs for lone parents—or to impose sanctions.'

She also disagrees with the philosophy behind the policy. 'Another factor is that it has always been a principle that lone parents will be encouraged into work, but that the final decision will be theirs.

'Lone parents can't win—if they go out to work they are seen as neglecting their kids. The proposals would mean that lone parents wouldn't be able to be at home with the kids at a difficult age when teens need a parent around. In two-parent families we don't bat an eyelid if one parent stays at home with the children. Sixty-nine per cent of lone parents whose youngest is aged 12 are already working and a change in benefit arrangements will just cause a lot of anxiety for no purpose.'

Peter Tatchell
Gay and human rights activist

Peter Tatchell is a gay and human rights activist and the Green Party's parliamentary candidate for Oxford East.

Peter Tatchell celebrates the fact that we now have a wider understanding and acceptance of families. 'The rather suffocating traditional view of families has been replaced by a more pluralistic understanding. Families come in all shapes and sizes. As well as the traditional nuclear family with a married mother and father and couple of children, there is much greater recognition and acceptance of extended families, single parents, cohabitees and same-sex families.'

Family structure, he argues, is not what is important for happy children. 'More and more people now recognise that what's important for children is love and care, not the family structure and the formal legal status of the parents.'

Tatchell thinks that generally we have become a more accepting society. 'A lot of these changes are due to transformed public attitudes towards women and gay people. As misogyny and homophobia have been eroded there's been an increasing acceptance of different models of family relationships.'

Economics has played a significant role, says Tatchell. 'With greater numbers of women entering the workforce, the traditional male/female division of labour has been questioned and gradually abandoned.'

He also notes that single parenthood is now a more widely available option too. 'Many fewer women have been prepared to remain in abusive relationships; they've left their male partners and set up home with their children. These women have taken the decision that being a single parent is preferable to enduring psychological and physical abuse at the hands of a sexist, violent husband or boyfriend. They also realise that separation from an abusive male partner is in the best interests of their children. It is not good for children to be bought up in an environment where their parents constantly quarrel and fight. In these circumstances, single parenthood is infinitely preferable to an abusive marriage.'

Tatchell does however also see negatives within these societal shifts. 'There is a downside in that we live in an increasingly individualistic, me-first, satisfaction-now culture. This sometimes means that instead of working to heal a fractured family relationship, people just walk away.'

And stability at home, he thinks, is of utmost importance. 'The number one priority for children is to have a loving, caring, stable home environment. This environment can be provided by a traditional two-parent family, an extended family, a single-parent family or a same-sex family. There's no one-size-fits-all rule about what guarantees well-adjusted, happy, fulfilled children. Heterosexual married parents in many cases provide good family environments—but not always. We are now aware that some traditional families also have a hidden dark side of domestic violence, marital rape and child abuse.'

Tatchell sees the New Labour government as having played an important part in these social changes. 'Without the election of a Labour government in 1997 few—if any—of the gay law reforms of the last decade would have happened. The previous Conservative governments were strongly opposed to the removal of discriminatory anti-gay laws. It's true that MPs from all parties voted in favour of reforms like same-sex civil partnerships and the right of same-sex couples to be considered as foster and adoptive parents. But that support was overwhelmingly from Labour and the Liberal Democrats.'

Legislation for same-sex civil partnerships has made a big difference, Tatchell believes, but discrimination still exists. 'Civil partnerships are an important advance. They remedy many of the injustices faced by lesbian and gay couples. But civil partnerships are discriminatory. The ban on same-sex marriage is a form of sexual apartheid. Gays are banned from marriage (homophobia) and straights are banned from civil partnerships (heterophobia). This two-tiered system of partnership law is not equality. It perpetuates and extends discrimination. Marriage is the gold standard. Civil partnerships are second best.

'No one would accept the government telling Jewish people that they were prohibited from getting married, and offering them instead a separate Jews-only partnership system. We'd say it was anti-Semitic—a law we would expect to find in Nazi Germany, not democratic Britain. Well, that's what I feel about civil partnerships. They are institutional homophobia. The Green Party is, so far, the only party officially committed to giving same-sex partners the right to civil marriage.'

Tatchell sees homosexual couples as being kept in a status which is second best. 'The ban on same-sex marriage symbolises the continuing second-class legal status of lesbian and gay people. Although I wouldn't want to get married, I defend absolutely the right of other same-sex couples to make that choice. It is deeply offensive to deny lesbian and gay couples a legal right that is available to their heterosexual counterparts.'

Not all, he points out, think as he does on the issue. 'The lesbian and gay community is split. About half think civil partnerships are adequate and the other half believe they are a form of sexual apartheid.'

Nevertheless Tatchell regards same-sex family equality as having progressed in this country. 'In terms of fostering and adoption rights for same-sex couples, Britain is now one of the world's leaders; which is quite ironic because, until a few years ago, we were one of the most backward and homophobic West European countries in terms of the legal rights of lesbian and gay people.'

He thinks that on the ground people are supportive of these shifts. 'Public opinion has been ahead of politicians for well over a decade. Opinion poll after opinion poll since the mid-1990s has shown that public attitudes are much more understanding and accepting than politicians have recognised.'

Under a Conservative government Tatchell worries that gay rights might face barriers. 'David Cameron is clearly trying very hard to make a break with the past homophobia of the Conservative Party. He and some of his key aides are evidently not homophobic. But their liberalism is not always reflected among the grass-roots party members in the Conservative Associations. Some gay people remain anxious. They fear that if the Conservatives form the next government many Tory MPs will not support gay equality.'

Tatchell sees David Cameron's approach to gay rights as being strategically driven. 'Despite his ambivalent voting record in the past, he has recently backed civil partnerships and gay adoption rights. I want to believe that this reflects a genuine, sincere commitment to gay equality. But I suspect that it is also motivated by the electoral calculation that homophobia is no longer a vote-winner.'

Duncan Fisher
Chief Executive of the Fatherhood Institute

Duncan Fisher is Chief Executive of The Fatherhood Institute, the national information centre on fatherhood.

Duncan Fisher explains how the Fatherhood Institute (formerly Fathers Direct) was established as a reaction to alterations in family life. 'Fathers Direct was set up in response to the fact that family services and employers were not connecting with the way that a lot of parents had responded to changes in the economy. Women's entrance into education and employment and the impact that that's had on domestic roles, for instance. We observed that state institutions and laws needed to be changed in line with these social changes.'

The organisation works on several levels and aims to engage across the political parties. 'We need consensus in order to be able to have an impact, so we engage on three levels: with local families, with the government and with the opposition, and with local family services.

'Both political parties are concerned about fatherhood. They're looking at opinion polls, for example, and noticing that there is a key issue. Both parties are actively thinking about these issues.'

Fisher is particularly pleased with the fact that the Fatherhood Institute has not become politically partisan. 'We're the only agency that is completely involved with both parties—we're very proud of this, it's very important to us.'

He sees differences, however, between the parties' priorities. 'It's not a Left/Right issue, but there *are* different sticking points for the Left and the Right. On the Left you have the focus on the welfare of the child but you also have a particular concern about mothers, so it gets sticky when you have to separate out these two concerns. On the Right there is more interest in relationships and that is more inclusive of fathers. Their sticking point is their focus on traditional roles—mums at home and the "working man". Having said that, both sides are actually pretty conservative when it comes to gender roles. It seems to be not so much a case of a Left or Right divide as a young and old one.'

Fisher thinks that an insufficient recognition of fathers and paternal responsibility is limiting parents' choices in the UK. 'People's choices are pretty constrained. Parents choose what's best for them in the circumstances rather than what they *want*. The nearest thing policy makers can do is to look abroad: do people take different choices if they are available? Only that way really can you tease out the differences between environment and preferences.'

Having said that, he thinks that total equality between the sexes when it comes to childcare, for example, should not be the aim. 'The idea of it being 50/50 in terms of childcare between mothers and fathers, will never happen. Nevertheless there is much more shared parenting abroad.'

One reason for this is that he isn't sure that men and women necessarily want complete parity in childcare. 'On average, I don't think that men and women would choose the same. The ideal would be that they were able to do what they want to.'

For Fisher, the priority is enabling choice. 'One of the things which is now being discussed is the need for more emphasis on fatherhood. It's a completely non-partisan discussion—a value we want—coming from the demands of social exclusion, changes to women's lives. What we want to see is an environment in which fatherhood is as important as motherhood. That would create an environment where people can choose differently.'

Fisher lists some examples where the role of fathers needs to be clearer:

'Birth registration: if there were an expectation of all fathers to have their names on the certificate, this would change things particularly for very young parents. It would enable them to understand the significance of a father to a child.

'Leave entitlements is another issue. Parenting share in the early years is massively affected by the structure of entitlements. There isn't a bias-free system—government and opposition have to play straight hand—do they or don't they want a structure that allows men not to work so much?

'Another issue is family services. At the moment engagement with fathers in many services is conditional. This means that the mum can get the dad involved if she wants to. The programme embodies the conditional nature of fatherhood. If the mother is struggling or endangering the child, you deal with it, but with fathers, you seek to remove them. A different directive would lead to different outcomes for families.'

It is on the issues around separated families, that Fisher believes the differing priorities of the Left and Right become most apparent. 'When it comes to separated families there are very different views between Left and Right. Everyone's agreed that child welfare is the priority. The difference is that the Tories want to go further in colouring in what the best thing for children is. Labour on the other hand, has taken the line "we can't say anything at all—every family is different".'

Rather than comment on which party is 'right' is his view, Fisher prefers to remain neutral. 'What we do at the Fatherhood Institute is to review the evidence: what do the studies say is in the child's best interests? That evidence does colour in the picture. So we would say: one, continued positive involvement of both parents is important to the child; and two, the system we have in this country makes conflict between separating parents worse, with the current systems of family courts and child support. We preside over a system which doesn't deliver in the best interests of children.'

Fisher sees making the Child Support Agency effective as being of paramount importance—as well as feasible. 'We could get it right—the solution is very clear—but it all depends on politics. At the moment the government's take is "let's bash irresponsible parents", a vindictive and unconstructive narrative. What we need is a system that combines robust sanctions with robust support services and to make the focus of our narrative the need of the child, not the punishment of the failing parent—we know it works abroad. But we are not prepared in this country to invest properly in the support side of the equation.'

Fair is not a description Fisher would apply to the UK's child maintenance arrangements as they stand. 'There are lots of problems with the post-separation structure: the model for benefits and services is a single quantum where one parent is the carer and the other parent ceases to be a parent. The benefit book, for example, goes to only one of the parents; family services are connected with only one parent; school reports go to only one parent. Child support is in fact the only area where parenting care by the non-resident parent is actually taken into account.'

Fisher refers to the headline case of a father imprisoned for not paying child maintenance despite having been sharing the childcare with his ex-wife. 'We need to re-visit the issue that, if the caring is being shared 50/50, do we really want a situation where one parent must pay the other? This case highlights the problem with a system where one parent is classed as an absent parent. Actually what most children need is positive care and financial support from both parents. This all needs a lot of work.'

In some respects, Fisher sees both parties as having taken an overly simplistic approach to paternal contributions. 'Today's paradigm is that the solution to child poverty is the amount of money that goes to the child: and therefore it just focuses on income. But part of the equation when it comes to poverty, we say, is the interdependence between finance for the child and caring. We would bring that into the child poverty divide—what does an imbalanced caring equation contribute to child poverty? Child poverty statistics, for example, are based on a child living in one household only, that a child can only be in one residence. That's a very narrow conception and it doesn't bring the child's perspective in enough.

Citing a host of successful examples, from Norway to some American states to some of the post-Communist countries, Fisher demonstrates that good policy need not necessarily be either Left or Right. 'In other words some countries with liberal regimes and some with traditional ones are getting it right.'

The Australian example, he thinks is a particularly good one. 'Australia has got something right in the sense that the child support system is good: it's radically about children; children are at the centre of the system. Here, we're obsessed with the adults and the conflicts. The Australian approach is "we've got to do everything to enable parents' needs—what gets in the way?"' For example, very practical things like medical conditions. When parents separate, a father may not have been the one that dealt with a child's asthma before, for example. In Australia they have a more compulsory system of maintenance which is both tougher and more helpful. It's a winning combination of "you have to get help".'

In the UK, by contrast, Fisher sees a medley of the least effective strategies in place. 'But here we have gimmicks and nanny-ish strategies, and weak sanctions and weak support.'

Crucially, Fisher thinks that the root causes of separation need to be equally addressed. 'If you ask any child, they don't want their parents to split up. We need preventative stuff, that's the Right's argument and

I back it definitely. For example, supporting parents in their first year of parenting. It's not about "relationship counselling" but breaking it down into the practical issues which could break down the harmony. In other words, supporting parent-related issues with both parents together.

He doesn't consider all interventions, however, to be positive. 'Hiving off the mother, for example, and not informing the father about breast-feeding is bad. That sort of thing is nanny-state intervention. We could do more to promote good relationships between parents. That is where the Right has the advantage because it values relationships more. If we valued the child's experience more we would immediately transfer attention to the mother/father relationship, whether they were together or apart.'

Returning to the role of fatherhood in policy-making, Fisher says he perceives a shift in thinking. 'Looking at the latest policy paper from the Treasury, *Aiming High for Children*, the approach is pretty radically different on the importance of fatherhood. And then there is the green paper on birth registration, which would require both parents to put their names on the birth certificate.'

To date, Fisher argues, family policy has not taken full account of the father's significance. 'There has definitely been a direction of travel. The fact is that the UK is pretty conservative and maternalistic—there is a strong emphasis on motherhood. This is very powerful and has led to a non-party political cultural phenomenon as seeing fatherhood as icing on the cake: if they're good then great, if they're bad get rid of them. The direction of travel is acknowledging that actually looking at the evidence from children, the fatherhood relationship is important—and so is the mother/father relationship. As David Willetts puts it, it's a sort of a triangle.'

He thinks that the Fatherhood Institute is having an impact in this respect. 'What makes me really hopeful about a shift in the significance given to fathers is that this is what mothers and fathers *want*—it's not pushing an ideology. We are really keen not to dictate to parents, about "what's best". We don't say that parents should share care more, for example. It should be choice-led but should give more scope—it's about widening choices. We realise that not all parents want equal care, it's about enabling choice.'

Fisher sees a persistent divide between the parties when it comes to family policy. 'I don't think that there is a consensus. Both Labour and the Tories have sticking points.' One example is adult relationships. 'All we can say at present is that the Right is more specific about marriage and parental relationships than is the Left.'

The Fatherhood Institute aims to be less specific. 'We at the Fatherhood Institute don't say "support a particular family formation", we say "support all parents' relationships with their children and support cooperation between parents to this end, in whatever family formation". This would lead to greater relationship stability.'

Differences between party lines, on adult relationships for example, are not necessarily a bad thing, Fisher argues. 'We think it's great if they disagree, it makes for more debate and gets people talking about the issues.'

Furthermore, as Fisher points out, contrasting policies from Labour and the Conservatives do not always mean different outcomes. 'Both parties focus on the mother/child bond and the maternal caring role and assign the economic role to fathers. The Tory focus on relationships does not necessarily mean support for fathers' caring roles. For example, the transferable tax allowance creates an incentive for parents to divide roles and this will amplify the existing pressures on families, such as the pay gap, to divide along traditional lines—and all the surveys show that the majority of families are frustrated by these pressures. Labour's system of leave entitlements, which render it more expensive and more difficult for fathers than mothers to take time off work, has the same result—encouraging splitting of roles.'

Sue Burridge
Policy adviser for the Church of England

Sue Burridge is Policy Adviser for Marriage and the Family for the Archbishops' Council of the Church of England.

'There are dilemmas for the Church as to whether to emphasise the religious importance of marriage or not,' notes Sue Burridge, Marriage and Family Policy Adviser for the Church of England, 'because of the risk of making marriage have no relevance to the non-religious. In a political climate where policy-makers feel quite nervous about supporting marriage, the Church is keen that its own support of marriage should nonetheless allow it to stay in touch with people who choose other lifestyles.'

The Church of England has also taken heed of the current political climate in other respects, Burridge explains. 'In my job interview I was asked by the Board whether, if given the choice, I would increase child benefit or bring back the Married Couples Allowance. I answered that I would do both. Up until now, a politically more "correct" answer in the world beyond the church,' Burridge adds, 'might have been to increase child benefits.

'Saying that marriage is a good thing is currently politically contested. It is not really acceptable now to talk about the health of adult relationships. Organisations working with families are now under pressure to focus only on children rather than the adult relationship, and the funding that they get reflects this.'

Although she understands the rationale, Burridge finds this guarded approach difficult. 'The government has got to be pragmatic: if we don't show an interest in later life by supporting the family, then we will have a huge bill because the state will have to step in and care for the elderly rather than it being the role of their spouses. That might sound horribly utilitarian, but it's important.'

The Church itself, she says, has begun to move away from adhering to such a cautious approach. 'At the time of my appointment in 2000, the Church of England Board for Social Responsibility was more in sympathy with the politics of the Left, supporting New Labour's approach, whereas now we have found that they haven't been entirely successful so we're looking back to the old remedies.'

Nevertheless, the Church is responsive to social change, as Burridge illustrates with their policies regarding cohabitation rights. 'The Church supports marriage but also calls on the government to provide support for the vulnerable. Therefore, we welcomed limited reform of the law to do with social injustice and vulnerability. In our response to the consultation by the Law Commission, the Church wanted to limit cohabiting rights to couples with children. We didn't want a time limit as an eligibility criterion because we considered this might add weight to the myth that as people live together they accumulate legal rights akin to those that apply to married couples and that it might create even more cases of injustice. So ultimately we wanted the decision to be one made by the courts.

'The Church was not in favour of cohabiting couples getting the same rights as married couples because people live together for many reasons—and because it would undermine marriage.'

On the issue of pre-marital cohabitation the Church is firm but forgiving about what is preferable. 'The Church thinks that cohabitation before marriage is not ideal. But the Church also welcomes people whatever decisions they have made in the past.'

Burridge sees the Church as entitled to play a role in public decision-making, something not all agree on. 'Yes, because the Church has a history of doing so, because it wants to help the greater good. The Church is in a difficult position though, because it is often either criticised or ridiculed simply for joining in public debate.

'The Church once had a huge influence on public policy. Now it is obviously much more contested. There is feeling in some quarters that the Church shouldn't use its privilege to promote its views.'

Burridge acknowledges that in practice the Church's influence has declined. 'The established Church has decreased both in influence and in people going to church. But this doesn't mean that people aren't spiritual, just that they're finding it elsewhere. Fifty years ago there weren't many alternatives. Other factors such as Sunday trading, an increase in sports programmes, have also played a role. None of that changes the fact that 1.7 million people worship in the Church of England each month.'

Returning to marriage, Burridge discusses it as a context in which to raise a family. 'In our view marriage is the best context in which to bring up children. But, we don't deny that loads of children do well in non-married families; we don't want to stigmatise families where the parents are not married. Christian adoption agencies sometimes allow single parents to adopt, for example.'

Parental separation is a great concern to the Church, Burridge argues. 'The Church tries to express its worries about family breakdown at every possible opportunity. In 1997 the Church made it clear that more needed to be done about family breakdown. The family was emerging as a topic that either main party's government would have had to address, whoever won the election. Up until the late 1990s few politicians were talking about the family, although the Conservatives were just beginning to raise it as an issue. Whichever party had been elected in 1997 they would have soon started talking about family because it had become such a pressing issue.'

Today, Burridge sees the political parties as having become divided on family policy. 'There is a significant difference policy-wise between Labour and the Conservatives on family policy now. It has become polarised.'

New Labour has focused family policy very much on childcare; Burridge is a little disappointed with the outcome of their flagship initiative, Sure Start, which has moved more closely towards childcare provision. 'I supported entirely the original aims of Sure Start. But Sure Start today is now about providing childcare, rather than supporting families. I would prefer a scheme, like it was in the beginning, which is parent/child-focused, providing things like helping young mums cook and learn how to play with children. There is however a dilemma in the sense that, economically, childcare is needed so that women can go to work. Family policy has got to take that into account. Especially as two salaries are now generally considered to be virtually essential.'

Burridge sets out the Church's priorities for family policy. 'The Church wants policy to focus particularly in two areas. Firstly, that policy is child-centred; secondly, as far as possible, to promote the stability of adult relationships through marriage. We do accept that marriages do break down, and we try to express our care for adults and children when this happens, but that doesn't detract from the fact that we believe in stable families and life-long marriages as something worth working for and supporting.

'My personal opinion is that advice on marriage and the family should be the soft stuff for the government, the rhetoric rather than in legislation. The New Labour government started off with this kind of rhetoric about the family but it has since stopped doing so.'

As part of its bid to end child poverty, New Labour has concentrated on alleviating single-parent poverty, something that Burridge supports. 'This is part of promoting child-centred policies. The Church is a member of the End Child Poverty campaign. Another of the questions in my interview for this job was whether I would take away lone-parent benefits, and make a generation of children suffer as a consequence, in order to break the lone-parenthood cycle. I wouldn't want to do that— you have got to provide. There are women who are widows; my own mother was a single parent for the very laudable reason that my father was killed in the war. Hardly any lone parents actually want to be lone parents, many want a partner. When parents are on their own for many different reasons, legislation is too blunt an instrument to control the shape of society in this way.

'There are many reasons behind the rise in lone parenthood; I don't think that the benefit system is really a significant one. Only a very small group of women deliberately decide to become lone parents, and that is a lot to do with the fact that they are unable to find suitable male partners to parent with. The need to educate men to be good parents is too often forgotten.'

Incentivising marriage through tax breaks, as a way to foster stability, is not necessarily the answer, Burridge argues. 'I don't think its re-introduction would be the right thing to do: it's a 1950s solution to a twenty-first century problem. Last year the Church was approached to move a motion in General Synod to bring back the Married Couples Allowance. In the end the church modified their motion to ask that marriage should not be discriminated against. In retrospect we should perhaps have pressed for more emphasis on promoting marriage rather than simply defending it.'

Although she finds it worrying, Burridge can see why weddings have become such a focal point in modern marriages. 'I think it's a new thing that young people spend so much money on their weddings. I think it's happening because of the changed nature of relationships. Because couples are often already committed to each other (for example, through cohabitation) marriage is now the icing on the cake, so the wedding has to be amazing. There is much more emphasis on the specialness of the day because of people living together.

'The Church tried tackling the cost of the wedding by promoting greener environmentally-friendly weddings. And M&S are now selling dresses for £100 to £150. But I don't think that these moves will have much of an impact—brides want to be a celebrity for the day on their wedding day. We just have to acknowledge that this is how it is at the moment.'

Burridge notes, citing Richard Layard's theories, that our interpretation of marriage in this country may also be culturally specific. 'Whilst marriage is seen as a wider social contract in the south of Europe, in countries traditionally more Protestant, the relationship between the two adults has been more emphasised. The quality of the relationship is therefore of great importance and, if this deteriorates, couples are less likely to stick together through thick and thin. If this is indeed culturally specific, we shouldn't regard it as inevitable—so it makes sense for the church to encourage people to think about marriage in ways they may not have considered before. That's why the church's public voice is so important: we try to help people to think more deeply about social relationships of all kinds.'

Esther Rantzen
Founder of ChildLine

Esther Rantzen is a broadcaster and Founder and President of ChildLine.

Esther Rantzen is cautious in her response to the question of whether children in the UK are happy today. 'My work with ChildLine means that I am disproportionately aware of the unhappiness children are experiencing. I'm therefore unable to say whether the British child is "happy" or not. There are certainly a lot of pressures on children today. On the other hand, there have of course been great changes for the better since the time of Dickensian children up chimneys.

'But even in that context, even given that we don't exploit children in the same way now, nevertheless I would say that one of the greatest sorrows which can face a child is parental separation. Some of the most difficult calls we have are from children desperate to find a way to bring their parents back together. Or the cases when they are being asked to choose between two parents, a horrendous burden for children.'

In terms of the calls ChildLine receives, Rantzen says that bullying is the most common issue today. 'The biggest problem is bullying. Thirty-seven thousand calls—last year alone—were to do with bullying.

'The proliferation in the number of calls on bullying has led to a very lively debate about whether bullying has actually risen or whether the explanation is that children now realise that bullying is not acceptable. I think it is more likely that bullying is more common. Schools have taken extensive measures to lessen bullying, including the DfES's collaboration with ChildLine to combat it, but bullying is on the rise despite these efforts. A school which has an anti-bullying policy, which all the pupils understand and are actively involved in, can deal with this problem when it arises. It makes such a difference if a school has positive policies and procedures in place.'

Rantzen sees several reasons for this increase in bullying. 'We seem to be a herd animal and perhaps we have some sort of instinct to turn on the alien and the vulnerable. There's something in us, unpleasant as it is, where the pack turns on the outsider. This doesn't excuse it. With each new generation bullying gets new focuses, like racism and homophobia, but this is little different from bullying the fat or clever child—or racism towards an English child in a Scottish school.'

Rantzen thinks difficulties at home can be a key underlying cause. 'Unsatisfactory home lives are significant contributors to bullying. I remember a recent call that a ChildLine counsellor told me about, from a child who had hurt another child really badly in the playground. It turned out that this child had never had a cuddle and had violent parents. One of the problems faced by children and teachers trying to prevent bullying, is that often the parents of a violent child are violent themselves.'

She also sees television as a contributor to bullying. 'I think television has also had an impact on the rise of bullying, with the advent of "mean TV". Before that no one would have dreamed of humiliating people on TV, but these programmes have glamorised bullying.'

Another change impacting on the lives of children is family structure, Rantzen says. 'There has been a big shift in family structure, with the number of parents splitting up, and the rise in the number of single parents, our culture has changed; my parents, for example, stayed together despite considerable differences. I'm aware that some other couples were to an extent trapped but it did also create a background of stability.'

The lesser involvement today of the extended family has also had an impact she argues. 'Extended family is so important, particularly as children can't always talk to parents about their problems. I had aunts and cousins to turn to in these situations, something which many children now aren't able to do. In my life my sister is not an everyday part of our family because she lives in Australia. Basically I think family structure has changed a lot.'

So has the structure of the whole community she believes. 'There's much less "street community" today. We've lost the little neighbourhood shop—you used to see the same people when you went to the butchers, the grocers... I don't see even my semi-detached neighbour from one year to another—we just send each other Christmas cards. The fact that we are so much more mobile today has also had an impact on community closeness.'

Returning more specifically to parents, Rantzen considers there to be an ideal structure. 'I am a tremendous believer in the strength two parents can give children when things work well. Having two parents provides children with role models. My husband, for example, showed our children how to use strength gently.

'But times have changed,' she adds. 'I am a godparent to an adorable triplet who has two mothers, one that gave the egg and the other that carried the baby. That would have been impossible 20 years ago.'

Another recent phenomenon is the rise of single teenage parenting, which Rantzen sees as part of a problematic cycle. 'I'm particularly interested in second generation teenage pregnancy, where young grannies are fulfilling both parenting roles for their daughters and their daughters' children. Teen parents are still children themselves. Having said that I'm probably just as antisocial as teen mums, by having babies in my forties. I have thoroughly enjoyed it but I don't know whether my children mind their mum being a little old lady!'

In terms of family policy, she hopes the strategies which New Labour has employed will be effective. 'The government has invested a great deal in childcare and like many investments we'll only be able to evaluate the benefits later on. But both Tony Blair and Gordon Brown have been very child-orientated. The NSPCC[1] believes in parenting classes—I know that these sometimes are derided, but how else can you help a child who has never experienced good parenting? Role models are absolutely crucial. No, we don't want a nanny state, of course we don't, but at school I learned more about the reproduction of the broad bean than the human being.'

To avoid 'nanny-statism', Rantzen believes that policy should focus on facilitating. 'It is fundamental that we support our most vulnerable families, not to take away their autonomy. It's also important that a sound infrastructure is provided for young people to replace the clubs and groups that we've lost.

'Research shows that left solely to their own devices, to roam, young people do not develop their talents. Some research we did in collaboration with BT showed that what young people really wanted was a safe place to enjoy themselves.'

She refers to a policeman she is in contact with who has set up two basketball teams in his inner-city beat. 'These teams have had a significant impact on offending rates, dropping street crime by 90 per cent. Graffiti and joy riding can be a response from young people not having the opportunity to test themselves. I cannot emphasise enough how important love and security, and outlets for their energy, are for young people.'

Generally, Rantzen thinks that we need to make more room for children in our lives. 'Adults need to give children time. It's no good saying all we want to do is help parents make as much money as possible. We had a distraught caller recently, for example, a little boy who said that he couldn't talk to his mum about his problem because when she got home from work in the evenings she was too tired and at the weekends she never had time because she worked in a shop, which was open seven days a week.'

In her own family life, Rantzen has tried very hard to make time for her children. 'We were luckier, we could set our schedules. When my children were young, my husband and I were very careful to organise our working schedules in shifts so that when I was working, say on a documentary for six months, he would be at home, and vice versa. Sometimes compromise is the only way.'

Rantzen sees childcare as very important in order to allow parents to work—but recognises that there are issues. 'My mum was a very able woman who had voluntary sector jobs but no career. There was no question that this was very frustrating. In a way my career, and my sister's, have fulfilled my mother's ambitions. My children, on the other hand, definitely don't aspire to follow their parents' workaholic example. I am not particularly proud that we have the longest working hours in Europe. I think we do have to look very carefully at flexibility in the workplace. Things like family suppers are incredibly important. I learnt the importance of that from my own parents.

'There is no question that it is a very difficult conundrum. I had terrific nannies, but nobody notices quite like Mum. The idea of putting a baby into a nursery worries me a lot; look at the kibbutz, they tried group parenting but found that nothing works as well as two good parents. Barbara Cartland used to say that she believed we ought to create a full-time parenting income. Maybe she was right!'

Rantzen doesn't think that a system like the French one, whereby parents receive a home-care allowance, would necessarily be desirable. 'We have to remember that France is bankrupt; I'm just not sure how practical that is. And I think I would have found the possibility frustrating, you'd lose out on the social element of going to work. Since we don't have extended families and street communities today, the way to find people who stimulate and energise you is through work. I just don't think that the French system is affordable economically—the nation needs the resource of female labour participation. But we must make it easier for parents. Quite a few of my friends have changed their jobs or hours in order to accommodate looking after their children.'

Gender equality in parenting is something which Rantzen thinks has improved. 'I'm a huge fan of the new man—I married one. Des—my husband—campaigned for the introduction of the BBC crèche. Are fathers the same as mothers? No. Are they equally important? Yes. Do women have the same opportunities as men? Not always. Although in TV it's sometimes quite difficult to find a man.'

On the subject of marriage, Rantzen thinks that we are increasingly missing the point. 'I think that something really strange has happened, which is that the wedding has taken a kind of priority over marriage. Every girl—and maybe boy—wants "their day" now. Diana and Charles' wedding seems to have given people an image of what they should be striving for. In my own case we got married in a register office. I put the whole wedding together in three weeks, our honeymoon was a weekend in a little local hotel.'

She sees the wedding itself as in danger of superseding marriage. 'What's the saying about puppies and Christmas? Well, a husband's not just for a wedding! Des and I got married twice, the second time in a religious ceremony. The second wedding was a public statement. It was a fabulous occasion and I would really recommend it. The government should make a law that no first ceremony should cost more than £100, but after ten years of marriage, every couple should get £2,000 to celebrate!

'But seriously, the reason I say this is because I think that marriage is the best background to create love and security. I know that marriages of course have their ups and downs and needs for compromise, and some can be violent and abusive. But as a society,' she adds, 'we seem to be going through a stage where relationships have a built-in obsolescence: it shocks me that they are generally regarded as having a sell-by date.'

As to what we can do about this, Rantzen is uncertain. 'But I think it is beyond government really to solve these problems. It can't turn the clock back. But arranged marriages have fewer expectations and this might well explain why they often last longer. Maybe the problem is that we expect to have romance and passion throughout marriages. But if you hang in long enough, marriage can be a great success—I saw it with my parents, and myself.' If all else fails, 'I think mediation is definitely important,' she adds. 'Adult warfare exacerbates fear for children. I would like to see a real expansion of services like Relate. Children, after all, should be our priority, their happiness should come first.'

Kate Green
Chief Executive of Child Poverty Action Group

Kate Green is Chief Executive of Child Poverty Action Group and was formerly Director of One Parent Families.

Kate Green believes that adequate investment is imperative to helping children and families improve their lives. 'Incomes must lie at the heart of the strategy, adequate incomes for children's wellbeing are key. But as well as fiscal policies to address children's immediate income, the government needs to invest in education in particular in order to foster life chances.'

The government must provide choice for parents, she argues. 'The state should ensure that all children are protected from hardship. But ultimately, I think that families and parents are best placed to decide what is best for their children. What the state should do therefore is help them to be able to make the choices that they want to, to make real choices. For example, to enable parents to make the choice to stay at home and look after their children, or to go to work, by providing childcare. Most parents do know what's best.'

Government policy around family does however need a sense of direction, Green believes. 'There are a number of different models that governments can take to secure adequate incomes to enable families to make choices, such as let's facilitate stay-at-home parenting, or let's put in place excellent childcare so parents can work. What's difficult here is that we haven't got such a strong strategy in either direction—there's a tension in government policy between child wellbeing and encouraging more parents into the workplace'

The widely-publicised Unicef report, in which the UK ranked poorly,[1] did concern Green. 'A little of the data was out of date. I hope, for example, that there has been some improvement in income equality. Nonetheless we have to be worried about the other measures of child wellbeing and we've got to relate these to trying to get a better balance between work and family life, for example. But poverty was a very important factor in the report's measures of wellbeing as poor families are more likely to be stressed etc.'

Green thinks that the discussion which the report spurred, however, has been very positive. 'What surprised me most about the report was how quickly it became such a lively debate—and a very good debate. I think partly because Unicef is an authority but also partly because it resonated with a lot of things that parents are worried about today. Plus we always think in this country that we have the moral high ground on child wellbeing, and I think that, most of all, people were shocked to find that we ranked below the US.'

Something which she sees as an issue in the UK, relating to child wellbeing, is the conflict between long working hours and parenting time. 'As the 2007 British Social Attitudes survey showed us, all parents want to spend more time with their children. I think that the importance of raising children and spending time with them has been undermined, and especially the importance children themselves attach to seeing their parents and spending time with them. The government has put the emphasis on work in order to allow parents to escape poverty but the balance has to be right and time made available for children to spend time with their parents.'

The UK's high level of single parenthood also raises issues, argues Green. 'Well, most lone parents never set out to parent alone. Therefore it is difficult to see them as having chosen lone parenthood when many of them didn't choose it. Lone parents face a much higher rate of poverty, which is why the government has been trying to get them into work, and to make work pay. The latest rhetoric, that not enough is expected of lone parents to be in work, is problematic—many lone parents want to work, but it's difficult to get the balance right with their parenting responsibilities, particularly because of the childcare issue.'

Cherie Booth
President of Barnardo's

Cherie Booth QC is a barrister and she was President of the children's charity Barnardo's until the end of 2007.

Cherie Booth learnt about Barnardo's as a child. 'But as a family lawyer, I became much more aware of what Barnardo's now do including, for instance, the support and advice they provide to children in care. So I was delighted to become involved. It has been a huge privilege to be President.'

She thinks children need to be more central to life if we are to foster healthy outcomes. 'A child-friendly society is one where children are cherished and protected but also have the chance to grow and learn. So it's a society in which children aren't pushed aside or hidden away, which accepts their energy, noisiness and general unpredictability but one, too, which has boundaries to behaviour and conduct.

'A child-friendly society likes having children around. So the best way we can move towards this is to listen more to children themselves, to give them a voice but also be ready to make clear when behaviour is unacceptable.'

Booth sees juggling work and childcare as one of the greatest problems facing our society. 'This is one of the biggest challenges we face and one without any easy answers. Every parent—and particularly mothers who, despite all the advances, still do the bulk of child-caring and household work—knows all about the pressures of trying to balance work and family. We may have far more opportunities than our parents ever did but, at the same time, the relentless pace of modern work also puts new stresses and strains on families.

'One expert said working parents feel they are taking part "in a controlled experiment in chaos" where one sick child or child minder or one dentist's appointment can bring the whole fragile house of cards tumbling down.'

Shortening working hours to accommodate childcare, she says, is not always the right solution because ultimately it results in lower incomes and lost ambitions for women. 'Many women have responded to these pressures by working part-time or deliberately choosing careers which make it easier to balance the demands of family and work. But they pay a heavy price in lower earnings and the country pays a high price in the waste of talents and potential. So it's in everyone's interests to help them.'

Booth thinks that under New Labour much has been done to address the work/childcare dilemma. 'We have seen real advances—for example in the provision of good quality childcare. I take family pride as well that maternity pay has been doubled and maternity leave tripled to nine months as well as paternity leave and the right to ask for flexible working being introduced. Many firms are also playing their part in allowing more flexibility in work. They recognise this as important both for morale and for the retention of good staff which, in an age where skills and experience matter more than ever, is becoming vital to continued success.'

Booth considers that we all have a responsibility to work on solutions when it comes to juggling work and childcare. 'Government and business certainly need to do more but we also each have to play our part as individuals. It is the decisions we take as we reach positions of responsibility which will do most to help change attitudes in organisations. For it is not just about changing the hours we work but also changing the culture of work.

'It's about looking at work practices, examining whether they relate to outcomes rather than simply are the way things have always been done. It's about encouraging people to work smarter, not just longer. If we do that—along with providing more high-quality, affordable childcare—then we will help parents and the increasing number of people caring for older relatives to balance work and career better.'

When it comes to identifying what children need, Booth refers to the six building blocks that Barnardo's sees as important to nurturing happy and fulfilled children. 'The first, and most important, is support from a loving family which meets the emotional, financial and social needs throughout childhood,' says Booth. 'It's a hard job, as we all know, being a parent but most fulfil these responsibilities admirably. There are some parents, however, who for a variety of reasons may require additional help, sometimes for short periods, sometimes for many years.

'There are also some 60,000 children in the UK who are unable to live with their parents and will rely almost entirely on the state, in its many forms, for their care. It is a real source of concern that so many of them end up in prison or without work or educational qualifications and living in poverty and we need to do more to help them and to support their families in the first place.'

Protecting children from harm, she says, is also hugely important. 'Last year, in England alone, there were 26,000 children on child protection registers. In almost half these cases, the main cause of concern was neglect,' explains Booth. 'The lives of many other children are blighted by physical, emotional and sexual abuse or by being witnesses to or victims of domestic violence. We need to do more to help them as we do those children who suffer the misery of chronic bullying, friendlessness or exclusion. We also need to step up action to cut the number of child casualties on our roads.'

A healthy start in life is also a critical building block. 'This is vital for them and for the success of our country. And while we have seen real improvements in the nation's health—and in the capacity of the NHS to help—in recent years it's still the case that the poorer you are, the more likely you are to suffer from ill-health, have more accidents and die younger. We have to do more to tackle health inequality which is why it is a Government priority.'

Strong bonds, Booth argues, are imperative for children. 'We need to foster a sense of belonging which might come from attachment to a community, faith group, a circle of friends or family. Too many children lack any sense of attachment which is something we, as a society, must work to correct.

Schooling is also fundamental. 'We all know that a high quality education has never been more important to children and young people,' she continues. 'We need to give all children opportunities to learn and develop their talents and potential. This is another area where the Government has made great progress with the results. For example, primary schools in the areas of highest poverty have improved at nearly twice the rate of schools in the most affluent areas. But we have to do more, including giving those parents who perhaps felt let down by the education system themselves extra support to help their children.'

The final building block, she believes, is giving children a stake in society. 'It is important that young people feel they can have some effect on what goes on around them, that what you do and say is important and that your destiny is not controlled by others who care nothing for your future. So we have to give young people a reason to participate, to perform basic civic duties like voting and to develop a sense of ownership and responsibility for their communities.'

Booth is aware that some of these building blocks will be more crucial for some children and less so for others. 'We do know that when a child suffers a particular disadvantage, the chances increase that they will be affected by others. So when focusing help on one area of children's welfare, we have to make sure we don't ignore other dimensions—or even, albeit unintentionally, make other aspects of children's lives worse.'

She thinks public policy is shifting towards the child. 'There is a great deal already going on, for example, to help families, including through the fantastic support that Children's Centres across the country are giving to parents and toddlers. But it is true as well that these are challenges for us all as individuals as well as for society as a whole. So we all as parents have to step up efforts to overcome the threats to children's health of obesity, lack of exercise and psychological disorders.

'Because of the incredible advances in medical knowledge, it is getting to the point where the defining modern illnesses of childhood in industrialised countries now stem from our prosperity rather than poverty.'

However it is not just protection that Booth thinks children need, but also freedom. 'We have as well to be careful not to exaggerate the dangers that face children or restrict their lives too much. For children to feel part of communities, they must be given the freedom to roam safely which means continuing to make our roads safer, to ensure they have places where they can play and meet friends and to feel they have as much right to be seen in and use public space as any adult.'

But, above all, it's about ensuring that we nurture rather than extinguish the natural optimism and creativity of youngsters, she says. 'Just compare the positive outlook for the future of young people with the far more pessimistic views of adults in some surveys. These young people said their most important ambition in life was to be happy and they believed a good education and hard work were the two most important predictors of doing well in life. They didn't believe their gender or ethnic background would prevent them achieving. Children, unlike adults, are more likely to believe that the future lies in their hands. So we have to encourage this optimism and celebrate their creativity, inventiveness and curiosity.'

Nevertheless, Booth believes that there is a single most important priority if we are to improve children's life chances: poverty. 'Despite the real advances we have seen in recent years, it's still the case that the single biggest factor limiting life chances of the largest number of children is poverty. That's why it is right that the Government has committed itself to eliminating child poverty by 2020 and why it is important that since 1997, 600,000 children have already been lifted out of poverty.

'If we can eliminate child poverty, fewer children will fail at school, have accidents, become ill, live in families that break down under the stress of debt and money worries, commit crimes and fail in school; and more children will experience the full range of crucial building blocks. So we all gain.'

Poverty, she argues, seeps into every facet of a child's life. 'Children from poor families are not just excluded from experiences and possessions that richer children take for granted. They are also excluded from the kinds of aspirations and ambitions which have the potential to change their lives. That's why, along with increasing educational opportunities, it is also vital we work with them to raise their sights and give them the support and encouragement to fulfil their dreams.'

Tim Loughton
Conservative spokesperson for Children, Young People and Families

Tim Loughton is the Conservative MP for East Worthing and Shoreham. Since 2003 Loughton has been Shadow Children's Minister.

Labour's achievements, Tim Loughton says, are very mixed. 'This government has taken a very belated interest in the family. The positives are that lone parents are now in a better position, and the new emphasis on providing childcare places is positive. But although they are quite rightly focusing on improving childcare facilities, the government is giving parents very little choice when it comes to options about how they care for their children.'

Loughton says extended schools hours are an example of the childcare strategy that has been adopted. 'This government has a tendency to dictate children's lives, for example with extended schools. I cannot see how this agenda—children spending more time in institutionalised care—is healthy for families.'

New Labour's emphasis on work is a related concern. 'The government has manipulated the situation to get more parents into work, and Brown's tax credits have coerced parents to return to work. I think that the emphasis on work has been a significant contributor to family breakdown.'

Family breakdown is something which Loughton regards as a significant problem. 'Without expressing any views—morally preferable views, value judgements—we need to take into account the impact of marriage and relationship break-up.'

Loughton sees one of the big problems with family breakdown as fatherlessness. 'There is a whole raft of statistics that show that children in families where there is either full or substantial involvement from fathers do better, for example, in terms of educational achievement and likelihood of mental illness. They are better off on a whole raft of major indicators. All the empirical evidence shows that fathers are enormously beneficial. There are of course bad fathers whom children are better off without, but on the whole they're beneficial.'

Loughton considers fathers to be vital as role-models, as shown by his constituency scheme 'Firemen in lieu of father figures'. But on the practical side, he thinks fathers are more involved today. 'There has been a substantial increase in the time fathers spend with their children, about a five-fold increase. For many there has been a great increase in caring, and an increase in fathers who want to be the primary carer. It's quite interesting how attitudes have changed.'

He agrees, however, that mothers do more parenting than fathers. 'There's still some way to go but there has been much change. The idea of a househusband is not laughed out of court now. Where I think there are real problems is when it comes to very young parenting, where it's difficult to keep fathers involved.'

Loughton is in favour of more changes to help mothers and fathers share the workload. 'One, where they want it, we should enable shared parenting through flexibility at work. And secondly it's all about work/life balance and the idea of general wellbeing that Cameron is espousing. Cameron is a very good role-model when it comes to fatherhood.

'More quality childcare is essential to enabling people to spend more time with their children. We also need to think smarter about getting fathers involved. I visited a Sure Start and a children's centre recently and I always ask how involved dads are—because typically only mums are involved. What the more innovative centres have been doing, for example, is inviting dads to run a football club. It's a question of getting dads over the threshold and being more "dad-friendly"—parenting schemes tend to be designed for women.'

The Conservatives think that employers should embrace flexible hours but they are against the Labour policy of it being forced upon them. 'We don't want to force flexible hours; extra statutory regulation always impacts on the smaller businesses worst. But where businesses are able to accommodate flexibility, the bigger companies, it can work very well and be a win-win situation for employer and employee. Big companies like BT have seen substantially lower rates of absenteeism, for example, by introducing flexible hours.'

The issue of non-resident fathers and the Child Support Agency needs careful consideration. 'It's a difficult area. You've got to separate out a debt-collection agency from the various routes that a government can use to encourage greater responsibility on the part of non-resident fathers. There are two types of non-resident fathers: there's a minority of fathers who bugger off who must be made to live up to their responsibility. If financial measures don't impact on them we need to curtail their liberties in some other ways, like passport confiscation. It needs to impact on their lifestyle.

'Then there's the second sort of non-resident fathers. Lots of non-resident fathers don't get to see their children despite paying full child support. Just because they're the non-resident parent doesn't mean that they're irresponsible but they might have had an acrimonious split with the mother.'

He purposely conveys a softly, softly approach to marriage. 'Our party has come a long way. Whatever forms of relationship people choose, the state should not interfere. But one has to bear in mind the welfare of children and the stability which statistically marriage provides. Personally, I think that married couples should be given tax incentives. But this is not party policy.'

Loughton thinks that civil partnerships should be more widely available. 'We all voted for civil registration rights. But heterosexuals are a class of people who missed out. What I would like to see are the most stable family forms: so that's one, married families; two, cohabiting families; and three, lone parents.'

He thinks that young people still want to get married. 'Looking at polling, most people still have marriage and settling down with a family as an aspiration. The imperatives to achieve this are affordable and accessible childcare and affordable housing, these are the two biggest things that stick out the most.'

He is concerned that marriage is in danger of becoming devalued. 'You tend to see young mums desperate to get married because their wedding day is the most important party that they'll have. The wedding itself is more important to them than the consequences of the wedding. It's very sad that this is the only way they can have a party.'

Something which concerns Loughton is children having to grow-up too fast. 'The teenage pregnancy rate may have plateaued, but ever-younger children are having children. Kids are being treated as mini-adults. And then there's the "schoolification" of infants, with things like the "mini curriculum" in nurseries and children being put into the education system at such a young age.'

He points to Finland and Denmark, where children start school older, as good examples of how to do things better. 'Kids there are way above us in numeracy and literacy, even though they start school much later. We must ask ourselves the question "are we starting children in education too soon?"'

He also sees the quality of their childcare as exemplary. 'In Denmark and Finland they have very good childcare places, and they go outdoors. Nurseries should encourage kids to play rather than being mini schools.'

He would be in favour of more investment earlier in a child's life. 'The Danish, the Finns and the Swedes invest more in childcare to save effectively later on: it's a false economy not to do so. We cannot rob Peter to pay Paul. We need extra investment in order to have higher quality providers.'

Loughton also praises informal childcare arrangements. 'Informal childcare is not recognised in the current system, despite quality childcare with granny being better. Parents should not be penalised for choosing not to send their child to nursery. At the moment the situation is very skewed.'

He questions whether we should be sending under-three-year-olds to nursery at all. He is equally dubious about the government subsidising extended family care. 'Should you be paying them? I'm not sure you should.'

Loughton has a measure of praise for some of Labour's policy initiatives. 'In principle, I'm a supporter of Sure Start, especially for deprived areas. But it's too early to judge how successful it has been in total. I think it's been positive in terms of early years health support and in parenting skills, but where it has gone wrong is that it is pushing independent childcare sources out, and also quality is a problem.'

Annette Brooke
Liberal Democrat spokesperson for Children, Young People and Families

Annette Brooke is the Liberal Democrat MP for Mid Dorset and North Poole. Formerly the Liberal Democrat spokesperson for Education and Skills, she is currently their spokesperson for Children, Young People and Families.

Involved with the Liberal Democrats since the 1980s, Annette Brooke notes how family policy has taken on a new importance for them, with the party bringing out their first paper on the family in 2006. 'In the past we have produced a mini-manifesto which has drawn together policies with particular relevance for families but this is the first time that we have centred a whole policy document on the family.

'Traditionally, I feel the Conservatives have been perceived as having a monopoly on family policy whilst we haven't given enough emphasis to our own excellent policies.'

The Liberal Democrats, however, are keen to keep away from what Brooke sees as the Conservative stereotype of the family. 'The Lib Dem view is that a family will come in different shapes and forms and indeed its composition may change over time. The actual family structure is far less important than loving and stable relationships. These are what really matter; one cannot say that one family form is universally better than another. There shouldn't be hang-ups about things like same-sex couple adoption, for example. What is important is the loving relationship provided by the parents and that the child's interests are paramount.'

Brooke refers back to former Welfare and Pensions' minister John Hutton's remark that marriage is the 'best environment' in which to bring up children, a statement she regards as highly problematic and prescriptive for the Left. 'I have always felt there was a common view between the Liberal Democrats and Labour, namely that the focus should be on children rather than the form of the adult relationships.

She is however aware of her own position. 'Of course it's easy for me to say family structure doesn't matter because I've been married for 38 years; as a practising Christian I personally believe in the importance of marriage.' Nevertheless she doesn't think that marriage should be a focal point of family policy. 'Yes, there are statistics to show that marriages last longer, but not all do. A better approach would be to put the clock right back, and put real relationship education into schools.'

Unsurprisingly, Brooke is unenthusiastic about the Conservative's suggestions to try and incentivise marriage through the tax system. 'I think it is absolutely ridiculous to do so. Not only is it insulting—to both those who marry and those who don't—but the sums involved would be relatively small for couples but a huge cost for the Exchequer, diverting funds from the most needy children.'

Brooke mulls over the question of whether marriage is still relevant today. 'It's not so long ago that divorce wasn't acceptable. In a way, perhaps it's more difficult to see why marriage has survived. It *is* still relevant and I'd be really interested to see research looking at why this is.'

In spite of clear divisions between the Liberal Democrats and the Conservatives on family policy, Brooke remembers noticing that many Liberal Democrat members were sympathetic to Iain Duncan Smith's *Breakdown Britain* report problematising family breakdown. 'I had a lot of calls from party members who liked IDS's report.' Brooke reasserts however, that although the Liberal Democrats perhaps share some concerns with the Conservatives, the big distinction is that the Liberal Democrats do not want to dictate family structure. 'But what we do want is to support families and help them stay together.'

Brooke is aware that there are socio-economic patterns when it comes to parental separation, but thinks that break-ups are something which people right across society struggle with. 'I can see that certain family-related problems might be particularly class-concentrated, but I think that the bitterness of relationship break-up is cross-class.'

Brooke sees elements of New Labour's benefit arrangements as unnecessarily undermining family stability. 'What the Liberal Democrats are currently looking at is addressing the fact that the benefit system has the perverse incentive to encourage couples to live apart in two residences. This isn't good for lots of reasons, the relationship, the housing situation, the children involved. I do see that the situation has arisen as an unintended consequence of supporting lone parents, but nevertheless it's really, really silly.'

On the subject of single parenting, Brooke says that what she regards as potentially problematic are the practical issues. 'I just think that it's harder with one parent. With a single parent you haven't got the same support.' But Brooke does not think that the view of two parents as the optimum situation is a legitimate one. 'We cannot say that two parents are better, that involves too many generalisations. Many single parents are just amazing.'

One reason she is reluctant to generalise is her concern about the unhappiness experienced by children and adults alike when parents are in an unhappy relationship. 'It may be better for the children in the long run for a break-up to occur. Having said that, I do feel that two people parenting potentially have greater opportunities to give their children strong support.'

Among other family-related issues in the UK, Brooke considers young pregnancy as a very pressing one. 'I suppose that teenage pregnancy is certainly rather generational in some instances, and the government needs to make sure that young people have opportunities through education. We need to raise self esteem and aspirations to break the cycle of poverty and also we are still very bad about talking about contraception and talking about sex.'

Other than the practical and financial, Brooke sees a need for other forms of assistance for families. She thinks the government should invest more money in counselling to help couples stay together, for example. 'Financial support is not the only sort of support families and relationships need,' and this is one of the reasons Brooke is involved with a community family trust. 'There are two groups of families that the trust worked with, which may have particularly stressed relationships but for different reasons: those with disabled children and those with a parent in prison. Keeping family relations together is very important to reduce re-offending rates.'

Brooke also advocates 'preparation' classes for couples. 'I think we should go back to the idea that there should be relationship and marriage preparation classes, particularly before couples have children.'

It's not just the relationship between parents which Brooke sees as important, the extended family is also a great form of support. However, she thinks that it is increasingly difficult for extended family to be involved. 'One of the problems about grandparent involvement with childcare these days is that many of them now work.' Nevertheless, Brooke sees grandparents as a vital resource. 'At the moment I am trying to persuade a housing trust to offer accommodation for young mums and others near to parents/grandparents wherever appropriate and possible so as to keep the vital support network together. Too often, with the severe shortage of social housing in my constituency, this factor is not taken into account and yet it is so important.'

Something Brooke champions to ease the work/childcare juggle is more flexibility at work. 'In terms of work/life balance I would like to see more flexible working hours. That is difficult to achieve, but we do have this very long working day here, and I do like campaigns like "Making time for children". The possible difficult consequences of having two parents working very long hours was reflected in the Unicef report.'[1]

'The Lib Dems,' she says, 'would like the right to request flexible working hours to be extended until your child is 18. There is already good practice out there, which should be highlighted.'

Brooke feels that flexibility needs to be the bottom line when it comes to family policy-making. 'Above all, we have to make it possible for people to have genuine choices, with things like offering interchangeable extended maternity leave.' She is concerned that many families don't currently have enough choice. 'For example recent research from the Equal Opportunities Commission showed that higher-income women are taking up the six-months maternity leave, which is something that it seemed many of the lower-income women were not finding possible to do.'

Extending parents' participation in paid work has become a focal policy in the government's bid to end child-poverty. Brooke feels that this strategy is limited in scope. 'I'm not in favour of a "one-tool" strategy for tackling child-poverty of simply getting more women into work. People desperately want a real choice.'

When it comes to parenting, one thing is clear for Brooke: the need for more father involvement. 'I think we need to do much more bonding with the father role, pre the birth of the child. Fathers need to be more involved right from the start of a child's life.' She thinks that securing a bond in this way would also help maintain better father-child relationships in the event of parental separation.

'Personally I'd also go for the "daddy month"[2] that they have in some Scandinavian countries, but I think again that's pushing cultural change, there has to be change on the ground too. I can see that progressive legislation has to be in line with social values.'

When it comes to New Labour's record on the family, Brooke considers it to be better than the Conservatives. 'I would always congratulate the government for the way it has brought in childcare, a tremendous achievement, but so much money has been thrown at it. I sometimes wonder whether the government has tried to do too much, too fast?'

Brooke also wonders whether too much dictation from Whitehall has hindered New Labour's achievements. 'A lot of the money hasn't been spent well, this may be to do with too much central control and not enough local decision-making.'

For Brooke, the importance of the quality of childcare cannot be emphasised enough. 'Poor quality childcare can be very damaging for under-twos—affecting their life chances.' Brooke thinks that elevating the status of the childcare workforce is imperative to elevating its quality. 'It's important that we do have a well-qualified childcare workforce—we need to raise the esteem of the profession and the professionalism of it.'

This, she recognises, needs funding. 'In an ideal world I would wish that we could have Scandinavian levels of childcare. But, despite huge investment by the Labour government, achieving this would need a massive increase in investment.[3]

'I also think that there may be issues when it comes to the government's spending strategies, that money could have been spent more wisely. Evidence now shows that Sure Start schemes haven't reached many very disadvantaged families that need to be reached.'

Brooke believes that a socio-economic mix is vital to tackling social exclusion. 'If you want to break into the cycle of poverty you need to get children from deprived backgrounds mixing with children from other backgrounds.'

She welcomes parenting classes, such as those introduced by New Labour, even though they have come under fire for being too interventionist. 'No one wants a nanny state. The liberal view is, of course, that the state shouldn't interfere in individuals' lives, but we do believe in an enabling approach. I think that parenting classes should be available to everybody, though not forced on anybody. I also think that universal health visitors should not have been cut back, and should be re-introduced, particularly to cover the gap of not having the extended family anymore.

Harriet Harman[*]
Minister for Justice

Harriet Harman is Deputy Prime Minister and MP for Camberwell and Peckham. In 1998 Harman established the National Childcare Strategy and introduced the New Deal for Lone Parents. At the time of interview Harman was Minister for Justice.

Harriet Harman has been instrumental in shaping New Labour's policy on the family. Juggling work and childcare has been a consistent priority for her, as shown, for example, by her role in the establishment of a National Childcare Strategy.

In Harman's view, dilemmas continue to exist around work and childcare, for women in particular. The nature of the difficulties, however, has shifted, leading to women having fewer babies, and later. She argues that there has been a shift from a scenario where women struggle to reduce and postpone pregnancies, to a scenario where women can neither have as many children as they would like, nor have them as early as they would like, the reason being that the structure of the labour market is restrictive. These new difficulties, Harman believes, are the price that women are paying for going into the labour market.

Harman also sees men's position in the marketplace as having changed: from a situation where men were the sole breadwinners to one where the breadwinning is shared between men and women. As a result, she argues, there is an expectation on the part of women that the childcare will also be shared, just as the labour is. In reality however, Harman perceives an expectation gap to have developed, where men are indeed doing more childcare but not equal to women's participation in the labour force. She believes changing attitudes to get men more involved in caring for their children will take time.

Public policy initiatives can help entrench equality in the workplace and she cites the minimum wage as a good example of this. The role of

---

[*] Harriet Harman has requested that her interview appear as paraphrased

public policy, she argues, is not to say to women 'get back to the kitchen sink', but rather to invest in women and improve their position. To illustrate the difficulties faced by women today, Harman points to the contrasting labour market position of a woman who starts having children in her early twenties with a 30-year-old who has stayed continuously in the labour market.

Attitudes and behaviour relating to parental childcare will take time to change, says Harman, not least because men's involvement in looking after children is a comparatively new phenomenon. In the past, men really only became involved in childcare as grandfathers—when they'd retired and were out of the labour market. In other words, men's involvement in childcare has been governed in the main by labour market patterns. Today, however, Harman sees men as having the chance to be involved in childcare first time round.

Extended family today is also in a different position—again relating to labour patterns. For one thing, grandparents now tend to be much older as women have children later. Harman illustrates this with her own example, pointing out that if her children had children at 35 she would be a comparatively old grandparent.

When it comes to relationships, Harman sees people as having more options today. She is not convinced that relationships dissolve more because men and women are fundamentally less happy together, nor does she see parental separation as applying disproportionately to particular socio-economic groups. Rather Harman believes that higher rates of separation are down to a positive: greater choice. Furthermore, she is keen to stress that in her view no public policy can or should say that every couple whose relationship has broken down must stay together.

Harman does however note that there are drawbacks when parents separate, especially for women. She points to the fact that when children are involved separation generally leaves women worse off, whilst, statistically speaking, divorced men actually become *better off* on the whole. This disparity, she explains, is to do with the cost of children who stay with the mother.

For Harman, as a member of the government, there is no 'ideal' parenting scenario. Longitudinal social research shows that having two parents produces the best outcomes, she says, but in her view the important thing for government is to respect choices. She argues that you can either use the power of public policy to back people up and help them in their choices or you can 'point the finger'. The latter option is not useful, as, she says, the Conservative Party has found. Furthermore, she believes that 'pointing the finger' leads to both missed opportunities and distractions from doing something pragmatically helpful.

Harman moves on to the subject which is perhaps most important to her when it comes to family—childcare. She says that childcare provision is finally becoming more valued. Unlike in Scandinavia where it has long been respected as part of pedagogy, childcare in the UK was seen as something that anyone could do. Harman believes that this government is successfully changing the image of childcare in the UK, as childcare workers become both better qualified and better paid.

On the topic of parental childcare, Harman thinks that we need to listen to what people want. It is evident, she argues, that people want to spend more time with their children. The government, in her view, should be striving to make this possible. Indeed there are many ways, she says, in which the government has been doing just that. She cites New Labour's tax credits, the minimum wage and extended maternity leave, as all having contributed to reducing the difficulties parents experience in juggling work and children.

Harman strongly believes that it is in everybody's interest that parents spend more time with their children. She rejects the view, which she sees as espoused by the Conservatives, that Labour has only just discovered this fact. She argues that it is not only important for parents to spend time with their children when they are very young, but also, for example, in the transition from primary to secondary school and during study leave in secondary school.

Harman is proud of her government's record on childcare. If you'd told her in 1997 that New Labour would go on to establish a National Childcare Strategy, with state of the art facilities, the doubling of maternity leave and a national minimum wage, she would not have believed it. She acknowledges that there is much more that the government needs to be doing, but she sees New Labour as having accomplished a great deal. The Conservatives, she adds, are under the illusion that they have contributed to these successes; Harman's view is that in reality they have actually tried to stand in the way of progress.

Today, flexibility in the workforce is a main priority for Harman. She believes that the government needs to change the relationship between employer and employee. Flexibility in the labour force is essential, she argues, and she sees the current situation as impeding flexibility. She sees the onus as being wrongfully on the employee to ask for flexible working hours, instead of, as she believes it should be, the employer being duty-bound to offer flexibility.

Having children is made very difficult by this lack of flexibility, Harman says, in situations where children become ill, for example. Employees get time off when *they* are sick, Harman notes pointedly, but not when their child is. Who, she asks, is supposed to look after the children when they're ill, especially when they cannot go to schools or nurseries when sick? The current scenario, she adds, has led to the perverse situation where parents sometimes resort to pretending that *they* are ill so as to look after a sick child.

Harman is dismissive of the Conservatives' family policy under David Cameron, describing their approach as 'Back to Basics without the necktie'. She concedes however that the Conservatives are up to a point joining in, as she sees it, with Labour Party policy goals. Nevertheless she sees the Conservatives' own proposals as poor, citing Cameron's suggestion of using 'exhortation rather than regulation' in relation to family-friendly policies. This proposal, she believes, would have little practical impact.

Harman is also critical of the Conservatives' stance on marriage. For Harman, marriage has little relevance in public policy. Moreover, she thinks that marriage has probably got no more public policy bite in it than the government saying that they would like everybody to be happy. She contrasts New Labour's position on family structure with that of the Conservatives; the main difference, she argues, is that Labour has engaged in the pragmatics, whilst the Conservatives have engaged in positioning. Harman also finds the Conservative position on marriage contradictory: as she sees it, on the one hand they seek less state intervention, yet on the other hand they moralise about what is best.

Nevertheless, Harman does see marriage as relevant to the twenty-first century. Her objection, she maintains, is to politicians telling people that they *should* get married. Most people, Harman believes, aspire to marriage, and want to stay together. She also thinks that children want to have a strong relationship with both parents, which staying together may help foster. She objects strongly, however, to the idea of any politician telling parents that they should stay together for the sake of the children.

When it comes to single parenting, Harman sees the problem as being that it makes parents vulnerable. She does not see socio-economic class as relevant, arguing that single-parenthood occurs right across society. As such, when it comes to policy and single parenting, in Harman's view, government's only legitimate role is to support these potentially vulnerable families. The priority, she makes clear, should be to focus on the practical issues in order to help single parents, rather than seeking to minimise entry into single parenting.

Interview Analysis

Interviewees were asked about their views in relation to family life. The aim was to cover broad issues around what they consider to be central preoccupations and priorities for the family. The focus of the analysis is to explore whether the views of those associated with a 'neutral' or left-wing position bear any resemblance to those views associated with conservatism.

Therefore the best place to start is by looking at the views of three interviewees selected to represent academic, political and religious thinking which is overtly supportive of the two-parent, married family: the conservative sociologist Charles Murray, the Conservative Party MP Tim Loughton and the Church of England's family and marriage policy adviser, Sue Burridge. All three are concerned about the 'changing' family; however their views are in no way uniform.

For Charles Murray there is only one kind of family: the two-parent one. Other forms, in his view, are merely 'living arrangements'. According to Murray the inherent inferiority of alternative arrangements centres on what he considers to be the problem with single-parent families: children growing up without fathers. Consequently, he regards single parenting as damaging to children and an arrangement which government policy needs to disincentivise.

While Murray is a strong supporter of marriage, he considers tax breaks for married couples—or 'getting paid to get married' as he refers to it—as highly undesirable and likely to undermine what he sees as the point of marriage: mutual dependency. Also undermining mutual dependency are welfare arrangements, Murray argues. In his view, social assistance supporting single parents is generating family breakdown and therefore should be stopped.

Sue Burridge, representing the Church of England, takes a much more moderate line. Whilst the two-parent family and marriage are considered to be the 'best' arrangement, Burridge argues that the Church acknowledges that many children do very well in non-married families. Therefore although 'family breakdown' is a great concern for the Church, she argues that it has no desire to stigmatise other family forms. Similarly, although cohabitation before marriage is not considered 'ideal' and marriage is seen to be the optimal context in which to raise children, the Church supports 'limited' cohabiting rights for couples with children, in order to protect the 'vulnerable'.

The Church has decided *not* to back the return of a married couples' tax allowance; instead, Burridge argues, it would like the government not to discriminate against marriage, as it currently perceives tax arrangements to be doing, and to support marriage on a rhetorical level. The Church's reasons for supporting marriage and the two-parent family involve both a desire to preserve the sanctity of the family and the practicalities around mutual dependency.

The only supporter of a tax-break for married couples is Conservative children's spokesperson Tim Loughton. At the time of interview Loughton expressed this as his personal view; since then it has also become Conservative Party policy. The aim of a tax-break is ostensibly to foster the stability Loughton associates with marriage. For him, the issue with instability—parental separation—is fatherlessness; less in relation to associated poverty or paternal irresponsibility, and more to do with a lack of a male role model. Loughton considers this to be significant to the extent that he has set up a scheme in his constituency with firemen 'in lieu' of father figures for single-parent children.

Loughton's problematisation of parental separation and support for marriage and the two-parent family are espoused primarily on the basis of research evidence; keen to disassociate the party's views from 'moralising'. Although concern about 'family breakdown' lies at the heart of Conservative Party policy, Loughton also outlines the party's issues with the quality of children's lives in Britain today, affected by both the quality of institutionalised childcare and long working hours amongst parents.

Ideal parenting scenarios, 'family breakdown' and marriage

Turning now to the other interviewees, what are *their* views on family structure, parental separation and marriage? The nuances of these interviewees are all-important, and their opinions on the three topics are often accompanied by caveats; nevertheless, overall, the commonalities across the interviewees' views are striking.

Starting with family structure, the general consensus is that there is an ideal parenting scenario: two parents where possible—and, on the whole, two *happy* parents. The importance attached to two parents can also be taken to have a wider meaning. Where two parents who live together is not possible, the involvement of both parents is seen to be preferable; and the sex of the two parents does not necessarily matter.

Several of the interviewees subscribe to the idea of a preferable or 'ideal' parenting scenario on the basis of research evidence: longitudinal research proves that children do better when they are brought up by two co-resident parents. Sociologist and author of the *Third Way* Anthony Giddens argues that family structure is undeniably important, on the basis of evidence showing that children do better with two parents, as does social psychologist Terri Apter. Labour cabinet member Harriet Harman also refers to research showing that having two parents produces the best outcomes for children but argues that government should perceive no 'ideal' parenting scenario in the interests of respecting choices. Novelist Fay Weldon is also not a fan of government dictation of family structures; however, she does think that government might supply relevant statistics to parents such as the fact that '…children without fathers do worse than children who have them around…'

Other interviewees argue that two parents are optimal for children from a common-sense perspective. Social commentator Polly Toynbee for example, who also believes that mothers generally prefer to '…have a man around', argues that 'everybody thinks that a child's best upbringing is two happy parents'. In *Independent* agony aunt Virginia Ironside's view: 'Two's better than one [parent], simple as that.' *Woman's Hour's* and Fawcett Society President Jenni Murray conveys her views on parenting structure by also arguing that parental separation is 'deeply immoral' if abuse is not involved; single parenting she sees as both avoidable today and to be avoided. Liberal Democrat children's spokesperson Annette Brooke takes a more forgiving line. While she is wary of making universal generalisations about couple parenting, she does feel that two parents *potentially* '…have greater opportunities to give their children support.' Brooke is keen to point out, however, that the sex of the parents is not important, something which developmental psychologist Michael Lamb and human rights' activist Linda Bellos also assert.

For three other interviewees, *Guardian* journalist and author Libby Brooks, chartered psychologist Linda Papadopoulos and ChildLine founder Esther Rantzen, parents' gender does play a role in their views on the traditional two-parent family. They each see the two-parent family as desirable on the basis of the complementary gender role models that a mother and a father can provide for children, as well as on the basis of the potential benefits of co-parenting.

For many of the other interviewees, the significance which they attach to family structure tends to centre on their interpretations of adults' aspirations—generally women's—and practical parenting issues: having only 'one pair of hands' making the situation more difficult, for example. For those interviewees who focus on what is good for adults rather than children when discussing parenting structure, the rationale is not necessarily that they consider the needs of the parent to be more important, but rather because this is the angle they are approaching the issue from in their professional capacity. Focusing on young women's aspirations, magazine editors Marie O'Riordan and Jo Elvin, for example, argue that women today have a very definite ideal parenting scenario: parenting in pairs.

From a number of interviewees' discussions about the practical difficulties of parenting alone, it can arguably be inferred that they consider two parents to be more desirable for *parents*. Child Poverty Action Group's Kate Green regards single parenting as an issue on the grounds that most single parents do not set out to parent alone as well as because it is closely associated with poverty. Similarly, One Parent Families/Gingerbread's Kate Bell makes clear that most single parents would prefer to be parenting in a partnership. Barnardo's president Cherie Booth is another example. Booth does not address family structure at all but implies that she sees *parental separation* as undesirable by arguing that poverty can cause families to break up. Equal Opportunities Commission chief Jenny Watson also appears to implicitly endorse the two-parent family. Although she explicitly argues that parenting structure does not matter, she sees parenting alone as an issue because it is 'knackering'—and is strongly supportive of paternal involvement, seeing it as both beneficial to children and important in relation to gender equality. Duncan Fisher of the Fatherhood Institute also resists the idea of an ideal parenting scenario. Nevertheless, in his view, preventative measures for parental separation are very important on the basis that '…[children] don't want their parents to split up'.

Along with Jenny Watson and Duncan Fisher, there is further resistance to identifying 'ideal' parenting scenarios. Activist Peter Tatchell is firm in his assertion that it is not structure that matters but 'love and care'. Linda Bellos is more tentative. She appears to see couple-parenting as beneficial for both adults and children, but is resistant to 'judging' models—one parent may have died, for example—and therefore more inclined to focus on the quality of the parenting. In each case it is clear that the 'prohibition' of parental separation and same-sex parenting in the past has been formative in their wish to be non-judgemental about family structure.

Michael Lamb also focuses on the quality of parenting, but with a differing emphasis. Lamb considers a relationship with both parents to be very important for children's development, however he argues that this does not necessitate 'intact' co-parenting: 'The bulk of the evidence suggests that children do better when they have both parents actively involved in their lives whether they live together or not.'

The idea that parenting matters more than family structure is an important point as it highlights two significant considerations. Firstly, the possibility that having two parents living under the same roof provides no assurance of both parents participating in a child's life. Secondly, the possibility that both parents can be sufficiently involved in a child's life in spite of parental separation. Parenting versus structure is also important because it highlights a reservation for conceptualising ideal parenting scenarios, on the basis that it is no good supporting structure per se as it guarantees nothing. However if 'ideals'—as distinct from universal truths—are the currency being dealt with, this argument need not prevent people taking a position on nominally preferable parenting scenarios. In Michael Lamb's case, for example, from his discussion about the practical difficulties of realising co-participation when parents are separated, it could be legitimately deduced that two co-resident parents are more likely to lead to the involvement of both parents.

In a similar vein, for those who do consider two parents to be important, there is an implicit—sometimes explicit—understanding that in 'ideal' terms the two parents are in a good relationship. In other words, the argument is not two parents at any cost, but that two parents are, on average, preferable. This is perhaps something which those resistant to identifying ideal parenting scenarios do not take into account. Similarly, same-sex parenting appears to be excluded from some interviewees' conceptualisations of couple parenting; an interestingly traditional interpretation.

Parental separation is generally considered difficult by interviewees and single parenting more complex than simply an alternative family form. Kate Bell of One Parent Families/Gingerbread seeks to demonstrate that single parents do not have different 'values' by arguing that: 'In most cases lone parenthood is down to relationship breakdown' and '...not a lifestyle choice'. The pattern within the interviews is to see the greater availability of parental separation as a positive, whilst recognising that the outcomes, and in some cases circumstances leading to separation, can be problematic. Women being left poorer and men better off, as Harriet Harman notes for example; children having less stability, as Esther Rantzen notes. Many interviewees who are concerned about parental separation on the basis of poverty for women and children and paternal irresponsibility, for example, are nevertheless relieved that women no longer have to suffer violent and abusive relationships and can parent alone without stigma. Polly Toynbee criticises the political Right's problematisation of parental separation on the basis that the positive of being able to 'escape' is rarely mentioned. In addition, several interviewees, such as editor of *Brides Magazine* Deborah Joseph, point out that the positive of women having economic freedom has led to a proliferation of divorce. As such Linda Papadopoulos comments that divorce can now be seen as liberating rather than stigmatising. However these positives are distinguished from the strains on relationships (including a culture of instant-gratification which Peter Tatchell and Libby Brooks refer to) as well as the difficulties faced after parental separation, from the 'trauma' of the break-up to the resulting practical difficulties.

Yet although parental separation and parenting alone are generally considered problematic, on the whole the attitude is that nothing can—or should—be done by government to prevent them. Terri Apter and Anthony Giddens, for example, talk of increased parental separation as part of contemporary 'structural trends', against which policy is powerless. Instead the recurring focus is on supporting parenting after separation. Polly Toynbee makes the point that if government has limited funds it is going to spend them on those who need it most, with reference to single-parent families where poverty is most concentrated. Supporting parenting after separation rather than prior to it, is based either on thinking that attempting to address parental separation is futile or that help is unwarranted as parental separation is a choice.

Choice is a significant consideration in discussions around parenting forms; few interviewees consider socio-economic class, for example, to be relevant to parental separation. In other words, only a minority regard structural factors—economics—as playing a significant role in how family life unfolds. Polly Toynbee and Anthony Giddens are amongst the small number of interviewees who link income to parental separation, both arguing that poverty is a major cause of break-up. Strongly related to the overall perception of choice is the fact that most of the interviewees are against the idea of government policy which attempts to 'prevent' parental separation; doing so is interpreted as constraining choice by being prescriptive. Even Fay Weldon, who is in favour of government informing people about the statistical risks of family breakdown, is not keen on the idea of government condoning particular family structures, seeing it as inappropriate for policy to take the 'moral lead'.

Is marriage relevant today?

The subject of marriage encapsulates interviewees' objections to prescription. While there is strong resistance to Conservative proposals to incentivise marriage through tax-breaks across the board (apart from in the case of Conservative MP Tim Loughton), marriage itself is perceived to be a positive by all who discuss it but Jenni Murray. Opposition to a married couples' allowance centres on the rejection of prescription rather than, as it is sometimes interpreted, of marriage itself.

A government privileging one particular form of adult relationship is both interpreted as illegitimate dictation of adult relationships and as an illegitimate declaration that marriage is 'best'. This in fact is a fairly accurate interpretation of the Conservative Party's motive for wanting to re-instate a tax-break for married couples. As Tim Loughton outlines, the Conservatives see a hierarchy based on the stability of desirable family types with married parents at the top; ostensibly their aim for a married couples' allowance, therefore, is to bolster the number of married couples.

As well as wanting to avoid a dogmatic invasion of private relationships, many of the interviewees' objections to privileging marriage are on the basis that doing so would not fulfil the Conservatives' ultimate aims. The view that the Conservative Party are attempting to use marriage as a 'magic bullet' to address family breakdown is common. The *Sun* problem page editor Deidre Sanders, for example, argues that it is not 'the piece of paper' that makes the difference between married and non-married couples in stability terms, but rather the type of people who choose and can afford to marry. Whilst Sanders, unlike some interviewees, does think that the government should help stabilise families, she adamantly believes that getting couples to marry would not have the desired effect. Similarly Polly Toynbee objects to the way Conservatives treat marriage as a 'glib fix-all': she believes that marriage can signify commitment but that it does not actually *create* it. Anthony Giddens articulates the same point by talking of the Conservatives as having 'fetishised' marriage, misguidedly seeing the act of getting married as the source of relationship longevity. He also shares a common view that a tax-break would not in any case influence behaviour and persuade people to marry.

Support for marriage itself across the interviewee selection is, however, striking, signalling a sea-change of sorts. As well as the great majority of interviewees being married themselves, in contrast to the association of marriage with shackling dependency and chauvinism in the past, it is, interestingly, seen to signify *good* (most notably, committed) relationships rather than negative ones.

Marriage is perceived to be a widespread ideal; in Linda Bellos's words the commitment of marriage is '…a fairly universal desire'. Apart from in Jenni Murray's case, it appears that marriage's negative associations have generally fallen away. Feminist psychoanalyst Susie Orbach, for example, talks of marriage as being fundamentally different today: to do with partnership, rather than identity and economic dependency. The negative connotations such as inequality cannot be applied as they used to be, argues Orbach, and assumptions about married partnerships can no longer be made. This is also a point made by Linda Bellos, who suggests that other types of relationships today can be *more* unequal. Virginia Ironside encapsulates the sea-change, remarking that she used to be a '…real 1960s piece-of-paper person…' whereas today she finds great value in marriage. Another encapsulation of the way in which marriage has come to be perceived as a positive alongside liberalised values is the introduction of civil partnerships: a strong impetus, Bellos argues, having been the extension of the right to 'marry' in the name of sexual equality. In other words, broadened norms have sought to embrace rather than dismiss marriage. Peter Tatchell conveys this point even more powerfully through his indignation that marriage by name has not been extended to same-sex couples.

In line with a general positivity towards marriage, several of the interviewees believe that marriage is experiencing a 'rebirth' of sorts. Libby Brooks, for example, thinks that there is a new 'pro-marriage' movement; even the 'left-wing and hippy' want to get married today, says *Brides Magazine's* Deborah Joseph. This helps explain why magazine editors Marie O'Riordan and Jo Elvin regard marriage as young women's ultimate aspiration in relation to family life. Although Elvin of *Glamour* magazine describes most young women as 'very traditional' because they want to marry, she says that those young women who do *not* want the wedding and the dress want the commitment of marriage. *Marie Claire* editor Marie O'Riordan also believes that the majority of the magazine's readers aspire to marriage, an assertion supported by a recent survey the magazine carried out. Interpreting the survey's findings, O'Riordan's analysis of marriage for young people highlights the way in which its long-term commitment can exist as an ideal after the 'experimentation' available with new sexual freedoms. O'Riordan also points out that with having to juggle work and childcare, a reality in so many young women's lives today, the potential longevity of commitment through marriage is very important.

On the whole, commitment is perceived as the motivation for wanting to marry, as well as the purpose. An insight into the significance of this commitment which interviewees attach to marriage comes through in their concern about lavish weddings. A fairly common worry is that the wedding celebration itself is overtaking the importance of the commitment (as Deidre Sanders puts it, for example). This is concerning because the elevation of the wedding is thought to mean that people are getting married in order to have a party rather than to make a commitment. It is interesting to see some interviewees in particular taking marriage's ultimate meaning—in their view—so seriously. Linda Bellos argues that marriage is being 'devalued' through an emphasis on weddings, for example. As a solution, Libby Brooks suggests that perhaps heterosexual civil partnerships are the answer. Male-female civil partnerships would mean that the commitment of marriage could be achieved without the pomp and ceremony.

Heterosexual civil partnerships are also something which Jenni Murray feels should be introduced in order to avoid the 'historical baggage' associated with marriage.

That the introduction of civil partnerships would make a significant difference to couples is, however, questionable. With the majority of interviewees not finding marriage's history problematic for its application today, a parallel legal arrangement would probably be superfluous. With regard to the wedding ceremony, with register office weddings available and over two-thirds of marriages today civil, it is unlikely that taking the word 'marriage' out of legal commitment would make much difference.

The Church of England's Sue Burridge unpicks the notion that the 'point' of marriage and an importance attached to the wedding itself are incompatible. In Burridge's view one of the main reasons for the wedding being so important today is that it differentiates married life from cohabitating life, in a scenario where the majority of married couples will have already lived together. Marriage by another name is unlikely to affect this equation. Today's general consumerism is also relevant. Deborah Joseph, editor of *Brides Magazine*, argues that high expenditure on weddings is just part of a widespread high credit trend. In this sense attempts to unhook marriage from the lavish wedding is unlikely to be successful in the context of a general culture of materialism.

The commitment between partners, associated with marrying, is considered to be beneficial for children as well as a widespread aspiration because it encourages stability. Esther Rantzen argues that she regards marriage as the best environment in which to raise children, precisely because of the association between commitment and security. Polly Toynbee also believes that marriage can make children feel more secure and Deidre Sanders that the stability associated with marriage is beneficial for children—although both are resistant to attributing this to the act of marrying.

Although the commitment element of marriage is considered to be the most significant, being able to *leave* marriage is seen to be fundamentally important. Indeed greater opportunity to do so has undoubtedly contributed to the positivity towards marriage conveyed by the interviewees because it allows for choice. Linda Bellos, for example, argues that one of the positive changes to marriage today is that it is no longer the 'prison' it could have been in the past, and that the '...freedom to end it, if that is the right thing to do, is very important'. At the same time, she is concerned by the casualness with which people enter into marriage—'...which [is] meant to be for life'.

Returning to the subject of choice, socio-economic class is something which only a few people bring into the marriage equation. Anthony Giddens is again one of them. In other interviews, class is alluded to, sometimes possibly inadvertently. Jenni Murray, for example, argues that one of the reasons that marriages last longer is because of the 'kind' of people that get married; a point which Deidre Sanders and Polly Toynbee also make. Looking at the relationship between social background and marital rates, the 'kind' of people who marry today are disproportionately middle and upper class.

Not all interviewees discuss marriage. Notably, of those who do not, all but one represents an organisation. This may be relevant as, although not necessarily the case, there may well be a distinction between the personal views of the interviewee and the position they have taken on marriage in relation to their organisation. Sue Burridge of the Church of England, for example, argues that '...organisations working with families are now under pressure to focus only on children rather than the adult relationship, and the funding they get reflects this'. Cherie Booth is perhaps an example; Booth has publicly supported marriage *personally*, but evidently does not see marriage as appropriate in the context of policy goals to foster child wellbeing when representing Barnardo's. Harriet Harman encapsulates this idea by likening policy involvement in marriage to policy involvement in the pursuit of happiness.

What should be the focus of family policy?

An area of the family which is considered to be relevant to policy discussion on the family across the board is combining work and childcare.

An enormous shift in parenting has occurred as both men and women now participate in the labour force. Whereas on the whole interviewees do not think that children's lives have become more difficult in the twenty-first century, there is concern that children are not getting to see enough of their parents. There is also concern that parents—mothers in particular—are struggling to satisfactorily combine childcare and work.

Parents need to give children more time, argue Esther Rantzen and Deidre Sanders. 'Boring time' where parents are available is very important for children, Sanders argues, rather than just scheduled 'quality' time. Both argue that having time for children may well entail financial and career sacrifice on the part of parents, and that this needs to be accepted; Sanders is surprised that it is not. This does not appear to be a common view and throughout the interviews the theme is that work patterns should be adapted *through legislation* to better accommodate children within work i.e. without career sacrifice. Terri Apter and Harriet Harman, for example, also believe that children need to see more of their parents but they see it as achievable through changes in work structure.

Before exploring the views of the interviewees, it is interesting to compare two contrasting analyses of the issues and solutions around combining work and family in Britain today. Professor Rosemary Crompton is a sociologist at City University and Dr Catherine Hakim a sociologist at the London School of Economics. Both have written extensively on the relationships between class, gender and divisions of labour but their conceptualisations of the issues differ considerably. Crompton sees one of New Labour's main achievements as having been to bring workplace policies to accommodate childcare on to the agenda. She argues that those women in the UK who do stay at home and look after their children are disproportionately working-class—that is, women with a low earning capacity, who might find difficulties in meeting the costs of childcare. In other words, although she considers choice to be very important, Crompton does not think that working and caring patterns amongst women necessarily equate with women having chosen them. She believes that working patterns need to change, for both men and women, in order to shorten hours and facilitate parenting responsibilities. At the moment, she argues, 'privately' shortening working hours has a detrimental effect on an employee's career profile. Crompton would like the government to sign-up to the 48-hour working week agreement and she definitely sees there being more room for workplace legislation to accommodate parenting and to foster greater gender equality in the process.

Hakim, by contrast, argues that legislatively there is nothing left to do to enable either gender equality or parenting in the workplace. For her, the career and pay gap between men and women simply reflects the fact that women leave the workplace in order to have children. Hakim believes gender equality today is a private matter and workplace policies are 'fool's gold'. She substantiates this by arguing that many jobs cannot ever be family friendly, for example jobs which necessarily involve long hours and travelling. To redress the 'pay gap', therefore, she sees the only solution as being women not having children—an option which she points out many successful career women have indeed chosen. Alternatively, she argues, role reversal could be the solution; however she does not believe that there is much demand for this. Although Hakim considers that men are much less interested in having children, she sees *women* as being the hindrance to role reversal in the sense that they do not want to give up the primary carer role.

On the whole, the views of the interviewees adhere more closely to Crompton's analysis than Hakim's. A main reason for the focus on accommodating children within work, rather than withdrawal from the workforce, is the noticeable emphasis on women in the equation. The reason for this emphasis appears to be that as they constitute the majority of primary carers, women would be the ones whose careers would be affected by advocating work-withdrawal for parents. Therefore, in the name of gender equality, work needs to be minimally affected. Terri Apter and Harriet Harman both talk of the 'cost' of childcare in relation to women's careers. As a result, they argue, women are increasingly having fewer or no children. The focus on women in legislation, to help them accommodate children within work, aims to mitigate these issues.

The Fatherhood Institute's Duncan Fisher refers to the UK's approach to the family as highly 'maternalistic', which certainly seems to come through in many of the interviews. This is interesting in the sense that it might appear to conflict with the importance attached to gender equality; instead it is clearly intended as an extension of focusing on women's rights which does not necessitate men in the equation. However, that fathers are *as important* for children as mothers is a point made several times. That fathers are more involved but not to a revolutionary extent, is also recognised by the majority of interviewees; as Cherie Booth notes, for example, mothers continue to do the bulk of childcare. Nevertheless the issues around paternal participation are generally not stressed in favour of pursuing legislation which would enable women to accommodate children around work.

That the purpose of the legislation is to enable *mothers* to combine work and childcare is not always explicit; however it is generally implicit in the argument. Not in every case, however. Jenny Watson and Duncan Fisher, for example, argue that non-transferable maternity leave means that men are currently thwarted from sharing childcare. Legislation to allow mothers to transfer maternity entitlements to fathers would address this, they argue. In a similar vein psychoanalyst Susie Orbach argues that men are not currently presented with the same opportunities for childcare as women; Conservative MP Tim Loughton believes that greater flexibility in the workplace would facilitate shared parenting.

Legislation generally entails a push for greater flexibility in the work force. As well as flexible hours, flexibility encompasses flexible working, in particular being able to work from home, job-sharing and shortened hours. Polly Toynbee wants the government to sign the 48-hour working week agreement; Linda Bellos wants the government to legislate for a 30-hour week. It is clear that flexibility and childcare is perceived to be the only way to accommodate children within working life without undermining women's careers, and thereby gender equality.

Several interviewees argue that the benefits of flexibility also extend to employers. Whilst there is acknowledgement that not all jobs can be done flexibly (including from home) or as job-shares, motivated employees and lower office costs (through outsourcing work hours) are cited as potential benefits. Nevertheless, on the whole interviewees maintain that flexible working needs to be statutory in order to be effective. Polly Toynbee would like to see all jobs advertised as potential job-shares and Harriet Harman would like the onus to be on employers to *offer* flexible working. Conservative Tim Loughton argues that flexi-time can also be very beneficial to employers as well as employees; however, he does not believe that legislation need be involved—a position that Harriet Harman dismisses as mere lip service.

That parenting between the sexes is unequal today is a widespread view. The source of this inequality is considered on the whole to be structural impediments rather than an unwillingness on the part of men. Linda Papadopoulos, for example, argues that the reason for unchanged attitudes to parenting despite huge social change is down to work structures not accommodating children. Papadopoulos also sees a wage gap between men and women as contributing to a continuation of traditional caring roles. That men earning more leads to women being the ones to take time out of work, is a view shared by several interviewees. Jenny Watson re-conceptualises the situation by questioning the availability of choices for *fathers*. Watson argues that higher average earnings for men disable them from leaving the workforce to look after their children.

Although compromise when it comes to work and childcare does not appear to be an option entertained by some interviewees, several argue that compromise is what women today would prefer. All or nothing seems to be an equation of the past. Marie O'Riordan's view, for example, is that most women today do not *want* to 'have it all'. O'Riordan's counterpart at *Glamour*, Jo Elvin, similarly argues that the modern ideal is the 'perfect balance'. A balance translates as women being both able to spend time raising their children and to maintain an identity and income outside the home.

The importance of women maintaining their own income is argued by Polly Toynbee, connected to safeguarding women's independence: keeping an involvement in the labour force for the sake of autonomy especially in the eventuality of parental separation. Cherie Booth is furthermore concerned about women leaving the labour force on the grounds of wasted potential. This concern links to an important point, namely the role of class in the childcare/work balance; an issue which Marie O'Riordan raises. Citing the dilemma faced by her readers—to stay at home and parent or go to work—she makes the point that it is a 'luxury' problem which not all women are lucky enough to face. This is something which other interviewees also refer to. Deidre Sanders, for example, notes that if you cannot afford to pay the mortgage without working the childcare/work dilemma is merely hypothetical. Fay Weldon makes a related but divergent point, arguing that the very idea of wanting to go to work more than doing childcare is in itself related to the privileged. Noting that not all women have jobs which they find fulfilling, she argues that looking after one's children may actually be more desirable than going out to work. Susie Orbach comments that looking after children can be stimulating and fulfilling. However, the lesser value attached to childcare in comparison to paid labour in our society is apparent in Weldon's argument. The idea that looking after children in lieu of a full-time paid job is a desirable option is noticeably absent. As Marie O'Riordan says, amongst her readers at least, opting out of the workforce is not seen as the ideal thing to do. The social interaction element (reference is made to depression amongst stay-at-home mothers), as well as the merits of economic independence, appear to tip the balance for interviewees in favour of women not staying at home for extensive periods, regardless of their jobs.

Although many feel that it is in women's interests to combine childcare with work, there is a parallel acceptance of parents who want to stay at home and care for their children. This relates to a theme recurrent through the interviews: the importance of enabling choice. Virginia Ironside is the only interviewee to explicitly argue that it is actually better for children to have a parent who stays at home post early-infancy—although Jenni Murray sees it as important '…as children get older' and Fay Weldon talks of children as 'suffering' in nurseries. However, the promotion of a stay-at-home parent is uncommon amongst the interviewees. Others express the importance of children being able to spend time with their parents—the idea espoused by Sanders and Apter that children need unscheduled time—but with the suggestion of accommodating that time within a working timetable.

Although the government is seen to be the key to facilitating a better work/childcare balance, several interviewees also express concern about the tension they perceive between the government's emphasis on getting people into work and child welfare. Kate Green of Child Poverty Action Group, for example, raises this issue. Although Green and her organisation perceive poverty to be the main hindrance to child welfare, she feels that the importance of parents spending time with their children has been somewhat undermined through government policy. This is important for children who want to see more of their parents as well as for parents who want to see more of their children. Tim Loughton regards the government's emphasis on working parents as a '…significant contributor to family breakdown'. Several interviewees do argue the importance of both parents working on fiscal grounds. Cherie Booth, for example, comments that women looking after their children are a loss to the economy. Anthony Giddens is concerned about the pensions situation for unpaid caring parents. Related to this, Terri Apter problematises what she sees as a narrow definition of economically valuable work. Apter is critical of the fact that the government does not recognise the economic value of childcare. Her suggestion therefore appears to be that enabling parents to spend more time with their children would need to involve financial recognition from the government. However, the suggestion that parents might be subsidised by the government to look after their children, as happens in France with the Allocation Parentale d'Education (APE), for example, receives support from only one of four interviewees with whom it is discussed. Both Esther Rantzen and Polly Toynbee, for example, argue that it is not financially viable. Toynbee adds that the government is unlikely to pay for a job that is currently done for free— re-asserting Apter's point. Conservative MP Tim Loughton does not think that the government should pay people to look after their children, although he does think that government ought to recognise informal—grandparent—care. Both points are perhaps inconsistent with support for government subsidy of institutionalised childcare.

Nevertheless, the general perception does appear to be that women would prefer to combine work and childcare, rather than forfeit work altogether. Flexibility as well as childcare provided by the government is considered the best way to facilitate this. Regardless of the amount of flexibility provided in the workplace, non-parental childcare remains a central concern. This is evident in the interviews. The availability of affordable childcare is seen as key to enabling families, and women in particular, to work. The expense of it in the UK today makes the government's involvement in childcare subsidy central to the discussion.

On the whole, interviewees are of the view that if childcare is good quality then it is good for children, and certainly not detrimental. With the aim being to help women combine work with parenting, rather than opt out of the labour force, the availability of satisfactory childcare is a top policy priority. Furthermore, childcare is not 'structurally' specific and therefore is the most legitimate emphasis for government on the family.

New Labour's emphasis on childcare has consequently led to a lot of support in the interviews for the government's approach to—although not necessarily the realisation of—family policy.

Harriet Harman argues that the role of government in the family should be to engage in the 'pragmatics'. Harman's main priorities, as indicated both through her interview and her policy record—childcare provision, assistance for low-income families and most recently flexibility in the workforce—suggest what she means by pragmatics. 'Pragmatic' concerns are very much in line with the interviewees' concerns. Notably, where the fairly sparse support for Conservative policy comes through in the interviews is in relation to the Conservatives' new emphasis on child poverty and quality childcare. Conservative Tim Loughton makes it clear that quality childcare, along the lines of that found in the Scandinavian countries, is a Conservative Party aim. However, there is scepticism amongst interviewees, expressed for example by Polly Toynbee, as to how the Conservatives would be able to achieve what are perceived to be Labour goals on a Conservative public spending budget. In spite of the new 'mood music' under Cameron which Linda Bellos talks of, Conservative policy on family structure is generally perceived to be inappropriate by those interviewees who engage specifically with the topic.

Conservative policies appear to be characterised as moralising or as Harman refers to it 'positioning'. As outlined, their new engagement with the more practical elements such as higher quality childcare is met with scepticism. The Conservatives' past record on family policy is manifestly affecting the way in which current Conservative policy is received. Several interviewees, Jenni Murray for example, talk of the punitive nature of past Conservative policy, particularly in relation to single parents. Proposals for a return of a married couples allowance are therefore regarded as a continuation of penalising the 'wrong' family form. In Harman's words, Cameron family policy is 'Back to Basics with an open-necked shirt'; in Jenny Watson's view it is 'Back to Basics II'.

Labour's bid to focus on the practicalities in family policy has led to a concentration on combining work and childcare and alleviating child poverty. These focuses are very much welcomed by interviewees. The extension of childcare provision, as well as moves towards flexible working legislation and child poverty pledges, has led to a consensus in the interviews that overall the government has a good record on the family. The Conservatives' concentration on family structure, by contrast, is seen as inappropriate and ineffective. Yet although the Conservatives' strategies are unlikely to successfully foster it, the two-parent family is in fact a very important component both of achieving better work/life balance and alleviating child poverty.

In conclusion, amongst the interviewees it is clear that work/life balance, or more specifically work/childcare balance, is considered the family's issue *du jour*. Childcare is not only helpful to parents but, when good quality, beneficial to children's development. Equally flexibility in the workforce can be beneficial not just to the employee but also to the employer. However, there is also room for a greater degree of realism in the discussion; both as to what constitutes true gender equality, as opposed to women simply emulating men, and with regard to the true extent to which work and raising children can be combined. Suggesting that children need to spend more time with their parents is often interpreted as standing in the way of women's equality. It seems to be saying that mothers should be spending less time working and more time looking after their children, as it is women's working patterns which have witnessed change. However the real hindrance to women's equality is surely this interpretation. If parenting equality were the aim then this would be a suggestion targeted at parents—mothers *and fathers*—not just women.

We talk today about the 'gender' pay-gap; perhaps a more accurate description would be the 'parent' pay-gap. It is taking time out of the labour force to care for children which constitutes the bulk of the penalty on income and career progression—*not* gender. If this were an issue which genuinely faced both men and women, perhaps we would be more rational about combining work and childcare rather than perceiving the situation as a gender equality problem in need of resolving. At the moment we see children as women's 'disadvantage'. We are expecting women to emulate men, when actually, in the interests of both gender equality and children's welfare, we either need men to adapt in the way that women have or a better division of labour.

There is worry throughout the interviews that children are not getting enough parenting time and that mothers are over-burdened. The trend of childlessness Harriet Harman and Terri Apter talk about is arguably testament to this. Family-friendly policies targeting women are only half the solution as they do not penetrate the whole problem. As Jenny Watson and Duncan Fisher amongst others point out, the government is starting to take more notice of fathers in family policy; nevertheless, the emphasis continues to be on women. Part of the reason for a focus on women when it comes to parenting is a resistance to mutual dependency between mothers and fathers, perceived as too much like dependency on men. However, when children are involved mutual dependency between mothers and fathers is fundamental to enabling parenting equality—by, for example, facilitating interchangeable roles. Social policy analyst Naomi Finch argues that New

Labour's election in 1997 marked a transition from a 'familistic' regime to an 'individualistic' one, in which women '...have the capacity to maintain an autonomous household...'[1] The intention behind this shift has been to move away from mutual dependency under the guises of extending greater freedoms to women—as opposed to an attack on partnerships. However, undercutting mutual dependency has, in many ways, led to women doing more work—and a one-way dependency on the state. Unlike in the past, mutual dependency between parents today is accompanied by much greater gender equality, enabling it to be a practical relationship rather than one heavily dictated by either a power disparity or gendered roles.

In order to move away from the idea of parenting as a constraint on women, fathers cannot be treated as optional bonuses: the proportion of families where fathers have never been part of the equation *by design*— for example through reproductive technology—is minute. Yet in a time when women can be financially self-sufficient and the state is asking to be treated as a more reliable co-carer than fathers, parenting expectations of men are low. The Fatherhood Institute's Duncan Fisher talks of both Left and Right as conservative when it comes to gender roles in family life; despite family friendly policies being seen as progressive this conservatism comes through in the focus on accommodating parenting within women's employment. The notion of women 'having it all' today too often translates as women *doing* it all, rather than actually shaking up divisions of labour between mothers and fathers. We can worry about women carrying a 'double burden' through the combination of employment and childcare or we can worry about men becoming defunct in the family. Either way, publicly— through legislation such as transferable parental leave—and privately, parenting needs to be a matter negotiated between mothers and fathers not just between mothers and the state. This is vital for generating an equal division of labour between men and women—as well as for generating parenting time.

The Survey:
Gauging Attitudes to Marriage Amongst Young People in Britain

Living alone, cohabiting and having children outside marriage have all become socially acceptable options, amongst the young in particular. This has not always been the case; prior to the transformative social influences of the 1960s—the feminist movement and the introduction of widely available contraception, for example—marriage was the only socially acceptable form of relationship, especially once children were involved. A minority within the elite cohabited but it was not widely acceptable. Today cohabiting, living alone as an adult, being a single parent or a divorcee are not regarded as controversial; marriage has therefore become a choice amongst a variety of options.

It is plausible to talk about an 'Ipod generation' today, a cohort of young people for whom a selection of lifestyles is (at least nominally) available when it comes to adult relationships. Nevertheless, as the interviews indicate and recent attitude survey evidence shows,[1] in spite of significantly lower marriage rates than in the past there appears to be a lot of interest in marriage amongst young people. The question is why. Now that it is perfectly acceptable to live unmarried with a partner—even once children are involved—why do young people who have not been affected by traditional norms to the same extent as past generations want to get married?

In order to address this question and gain an understanding of what marriage signifies to young people today, Civitas commissioned Ipsos MORI to survey young people in Britain's attitudes to marriage using four weeks on their omnibus survey, Capibus.[2] A population of 1,560 British men and women (of all marital statuses) between the ages of 20 and 35 years-old were asked about their personal attitudes to marriage.

The survey has three main segments. The initial segment of the survey focuses on whether respondents want to marry. The first aim is to establish the percentages of unmarried people within the given age range who think that they would like to get married one day, those who think that they would not like to marry and those who do not have a view. Ipsos MORI has broken the responses down into several demographic sub-categories of which the following have been incorporated into the analysis: sex, age, socio-economic class, relationship status and parenting status. These sub-categories allow for an exploration of patterns between respondents' demographic characteristics and their responses. For example, sub-categorisation enables us to see if greater numbers of one sex or the other, or one age group than another, would like to marry.

The next step in the survey is to understand the motivation of those respondents who express an interest in marriage—or have married: what is/was their main reason for wanting to marry? Security, commitment, inheritance tax or perhaps a desire to maintain tradition? Here analysis of the sub-categories allows us to see, for example, why those cohabiting might aspire to marriage and thereby how they perceive marriage to differ from living together.

The third aim is to determine whether young people have preconditions for marriage, and if so what they are. Are some people in the survey who aspire to getting married held back from doing so? If so, are their reasons for postponement predominantly positive, such as enjoying personal freedom or wanting to get to know their partner better, or are there financial and practical constraints creating hurdles? With this question the sub-categories allow for analysis of the responses by socio-economic class. This is particularly useful in gaining an understanding of whether different classes face different issues when it comes to getting married, or indeed whether different socio-economic groups have different preconditions for when they marry.

The next part of the survey looks at those young people who do not want to marry. The aim is to try to get an idea of what these respondents think about marriage by looking at the answers they give for not wanting to get married. Of particular interest is determining whether those who do not want to marry have negative views about marriage per se or simply think it unnecessary. Alternatively, perhaps they are resistant to the idea of entering into a legal relationship. The sub-categories again help provide an insight into who, in terms of demographics, thinks what in the survey findings. Are the youngest age group disproportionately represented, for example, amongst those who feel that marriage is outdated?

Finally, at the end of the survey, two replica questions taken from the British Social Attitudes Survey have been presented to all respondents. These questions do not relate to personal aspirations and circumstance but instead gauge a 'generalising' view. The reason for putting these replica questions in is to see whether respondents' personal views in relation to marriage—what they want for themselves—differ from their views about marriage more generally. Ipsos MORI has processed the data so that the corresponding personal and general questions can be compared.

In terms of the survey's format, respondents have been shown a range of responses to choose from rather than being asked open-ended questions. This style of questioning is particularly suitable for a survey which involves both a sensitive topic and, as the pilot surveying revealed, a topic which some people find difficult to articulate their feelings about unprompted. The piloting stage, carried out amongst a non-random selection of thirty men and women between the ages of 20 and 35, helped build sets of responses which covered the most commonly sought answers. Test runs of different forms of the survey also helped fine-tune the questions and response options for clarity.

Survey conclusions

The survey results show that the majority of young people—70 per cent—in the UK today would like to marry one day. The high level of interest in marriage amongst those surveyed mirrors the conclusions of previous research in recent years.[3] Respondents' main reason for wanting to marry is commitment, with reasons which might have been the main motivations in the past—social acceptability, tradition and religion, for example—much less important today. This 'de-institutionalised' conceptualisation of marriage resonates strongly with the views of the interviewees.

Less pressure to marry has unambiguously affected marriage rates, but notably it has not led to the end of marriage as a widespread ideal. It might even be argued that marriage is *more* idealised today than ever before, both in light of its popularity without the coercion of normative pressure and because, as will be discussed, for many marriage appears to require preconditions which people do not always feel can be fulfilled. Fewer people marry today and divorce has increased, as not being married has ceased to carry the same social penalties as in the past. The survey findings demonstrate that nevertheless, for the majority of young people, marriage has a differentiating significance from other forms of adult relationships. (This is consistent with survey evidence which has found that a minority of the young consider marriage to be irrelevant today.[4]) Illustrating this differentiating significance and one of the most interesting findings in the survey is the fact that marriage is most popular amongst cohabiting respondents. Although it is socially acceptable to live together unmarried in Britain today, the survey shows that formalising a relationship through marriage is a widely held aspiration.

Marriage's popularity amongst cohabitees in the survey contributes to a body of evidence illustrating the way in which marriage is perceived as a progression, rather than a deviation, from living together. Ernestina Coast of the London School of Economics, for example, has analysed the marital aspirations of young people surveyed in the British Household Panel Survey. She has found that when asked about their future intentions, three-quarters of men and women reported that they were either planning, or expected, to get married.[5] Swedish data reveals similar attitudes. Sociologist Eva Bernhardt has found that for Swedes marriage is also the majority aspiration amongst cohabiting young people, which is significant in light of Sweden's progressiveness. Analysis of couples' attitudes to marriage leads Bernhardt to conclude that '…an overwhelming majority of young cohabiting couples in Sweden expect to get married'.[6]

Rather than rendering marriage redundant, the availability of alternative relationship options appears to have generated new trajectories. With cohabitation this is important because it demonstrates the way in which, in the majority of cases, living together unmarried and getting married are not mutually exclusive, but complementary processes. It also highlights a distinction between cohabitation and marriage, in more than legal status. In the main, cohabitation is not replacing marriage; it may be *dis*placing it, in the sense that people no longer have to marry in order to have a live-in relationship, contributing to lower marriage rates. Yet significantly, the rise of cohabitation does not equate with a disinterest in the formalised commitment of marriage. With by far the most popular reason for wanting to marry in the survey being to commit to one's partner, it is clear that marriage is perceived to be distinctive.

If marriage signifies commitment and the majority of young people want to marry one day, this suggests that a desire for continual fluidity in personal relationships is not an accurate depiction of 'modern' ideals. Instead, as part of new relationship 'trajectories', marriage is perceived as *following* a period of relational experimentation and fluidity. This aspiration for long-term relationships connects to the second most popular reason for wanting to marry: in order to raise children within marriage. Looking at the reasons chosen for wanting to have children within marriage, the most popular is a perception of greater stability. Commitment between parents and stability for children clearly complement each other.

The most popular reasons for not yet having married (amongst those who want to) add to a perception of marriage as an enduring commitment. The two most commonly chosen reasons for waiting are not having met someone they want to marry and enjoying their current freedom. Both these answers imply that getting married is a long-term plan which requires wanting to make a commitment, both in terms of lifestyle and choice of partner. For cohabiting respondents, not having met the right person is least popular as a main reason for postponing marriage. This is likely to be the case as many cohabiting respondents will be living together with the person they would like to marry, reiterating the notion of marriage as the next step after cohabitation. Looking at the most frequently chosen responses for waiting to marry, this next step involves largely practical preconditions for cohabitees.

On top of the widespread interest in getting married in the survey findings, and in particular the fact that the youngest age group want to marry the most, little sense of the animosity towards marriage which might have been expressed by young people in the past is reflected in the views of those respondents who said that they did *not* want to marry.

Regarded by feminists as the home of female oppression, in the 1970s Germaine Greer famously branded married life 'a legalised form of slavery' for women.[7] Politically and economically, women had been subordinate to men, and the dynamics of marriage were thought to perpetuate this inequality. Financial reliance on male breadwinners made marriage synonymous with dependency on men. Together with rigid divorce laws, this dependency made it difficult for women to leave marriages. One way to reject male dominance was to also reject marriage. For a long time afterwards, marriage was considered to be fundamentally at odds with women's emancipation. What is evident today is that marriage has been extricated from gender inequality. Greater equality between the sexes has entailed women participating in public life to a greater extent through education and employment, rather than by not marrying.

Very much in line with the sea-change apparent in the interviewees, the findings of the survey indicate that culturally we have moved on from the idea of marriage as the negative encapsulated by Greer, as we have progressed on gender equality. This is evident by the high proportion of young people aspiring to marriage, the comparatively low proportion who do not want to marry, and the reasons chosen for not wanting to marry. Furthermore very few respondents in the survey do not want to marry because they regard it is as being problematic for equality between men and women.

The percentage of respondents in the survey who expressed no desire to marry is small: 200 out of 1,070 (18 per cent). It is important to note that due to the small number of respondents involved, once the sample is broken down by demographics any conclusions can only be tentative; for assertions rather than suggestions to be made, the size of the sample who do not want to marry would need to be substantially larger.

Other than marriage's evident popularity, one reason for the particularly small size of this group is that a fairly high proportion (12 per cent) of those who have not said that they want to marry have opted for 'don't have a view' rather than rejecting the possibility altogether. The most popular reasons for not aspiring to marriage also suggest more ambivalence than negativity towards it. On the whole, the reasons selected for not wanting to get married relate to the idea of marriage as superfluous; the most popular reason being that they are happy in their current situation. That these are the principal reasons for not wanting to get married fits in with a more personal and less institutional model of marriage today. If getting married is largely seen as a way of expressing commitment, it is logical that some people feel commitment is a possibility without the formalities of marriage.

This is one interpretation of why some respondents might not want to marry. Another interpretation is that marriage *does* represent a distinctive commitment to some of those who do not want to marry. Although marriage may be an ideal, these respondents may not see marriage as available to them. The possibility that this is the case for some of those apparently not interested in marriage relates to what we know about their demographic profiles. Linking past research on the backgrounds of those likely to marry with the demographic profiles in the survey of those who have said that they would not like to marry points towards an argument of aspirations adapted to circumstance.

Breaking down the data from the survey by sex, age, socio-economic class, parenting and relationship statuses, some patterns emerge (see Appendix 2). It is important to re-iterate however that the small number of respondents within the survey's population who have said that they do not want to marry means that the results are not necessarily nationally representative, and that patterns emergent from these findings may not necessarily be applicable to the general population. Nevertheless, the available data provides some valuable insights from which propositions can be made.

Women for example are considerably more likely to not want to marry than men. The sub-categorisations of the responses can be used to unpick this disparity between the sexes. When the population is broken down according to demographics, reasons behind the gender difference on this question become clearer. Cross-referencing both backgrounds and responses, women are considerably more likely to be in three out of the five sub-categories which are most likely to not want to marry. Women are more likely to be parents, to be separated, and to be in the lowest social class category. Why are these groups less likely to want to marry?

The link between the groups who are less inclined to marry—although this cannot be proven to be the case—may be a lesser level of idealism due to circumstance. The common thread between the sub-categories which are most likely to not want to marry is lower socio-economic status, gauged by social grade category and education level. Women, parents and separated respondents are more likely to be in the lowest social class category and/or have no qualifications than their counterparts. Similarly, out of the three age groups, the highest number of respondents with no qualifications is in the eldest group.

A significant body of research has identified a strong connection between lower marriage rates and lower socio-economic class:

> Several qualitative and quantitative studies have demonstrated that while marriage is valued and respected among the poor (Bulcroft and Bulcroft, 1993; Carlson, McLanahan and England, 2001; Harknett and McLanahan, 2001; Tucker and Mitchell-Kernan, 1995), economic factors play a central role in when and if marriages occur. Both men and women seek partners who have a solid education and good, stable employment.[8]

Sociological evidence from the United States suggests that lower marriage rates amongst those on lower incomes do not necessarily signify less value attached to marriage. On the contrary, marriage may be held in such high esteem, requiring a set of prerequisites so ambitious, that it is considered unrealistic. Sociologist Kathryn Edin argues that marriage is increasingly viewed as a 'luxury good' and therefore outside the economic reach of low-income couples as '…disadvantaged men and women hold marriage to an economic standard that demands a fairly high level of financial stability—enough to accumulate significant common assets'.[9]

This may mean that marriage drops off the agenda of those on lower incomes. Behaviour-wise, research from the Economic and Social Research Council (ESRC) shows the way in which, once children are involved, cohabitation instead of marriage is strongly connected to income in Britain. Using data from the 2001 Census, the ESRC found that the geography of unmarried parents is very closely linked to local economy and social class. The data revealed that the areas in Britain where cohabitation with children is most prevalent are the poorest areas '…with the highest proportions of working-class parents…' and areas '…notorious for the economic breakdown of once thriving working-class industries…' The 'prime examples' are former steel and coal regions such as South Yorkshire, Lincolnshire and Nottinghamshire. In contrast, the authors note, '…the most prosperous areas with high numbers of middle-class families stick to marriage when having children'.[10]

Both sets of research help to clarify a seeming contradiction between valuing marriage whilst opting out of it. Similarly, the findings from the survey do not necessarily indicate that marriage is not valued by those in the lower socio-economic classes, but that it may be perceived to be outside their reach. Although it may seem to be a misinterpretation to extrapolate from respondents who have unambiguously said that they *do not want to marry*, that they may actually idealise marriage, the relationship between socio-economic class and a negative response to getting married is plausibly related to perceptions of the availability of marriage.

From looking at both the responses of those who want to marry and those who do not, marriage appears to be very much an ideal in twenty-first century Britain. Marriage has, therefore, moved from being a social norm, to being problematised by feminism, to becoming a personal aspiration. The private significance of marriage today helps to explain why only 20 per cent of those respondents in the survey who would like to get married think that married people generally are happier. Equally it explains why fewer than half of those respondents who want to marry think that people who have children ought to marry (41 per cent). Similarly, only 30 per cent of respondents who want to marry in order to have children within marriage think that people who have children, ought to marry. In other words, the divergence between responses to the 'generalising' questions of the British Social Attitudes Survey (BSA) and respondents' personal aspirations reveal important differences. The latest BSA results highlight the co-existence in Britain today of personal aspirations towards marriage and liberalised social norms. The results of the 24th survey, which is based on questioning the population in 2007, show that: 'Two-thirds (66 per cent) of the population think there is little difference socially between being married and living together.' The authors of the BSA analysis on contemporary attitudes to relationships conclude that: 'The latest annual British Social Attitudes report confirms that people's views on marriage are more liberal than they were 20 years ago.'[11]

These divergences emphasise the contemporary delineation between personal aspirations and social norms. An ambivalence about *other* people and marriage, as shown in the latest BSA, is often interpreted as a modern ambivalence towards getting married oneself. The findings on personal attitudes towards marriage show this to be a misreading.

The Survey: Findings in Full

1. Question: Do you think you would like to get married one day?

Having established who is already married within the sample, this question has been asked to all the 20-35 year-olds who are not married. The aim of this question is to gauge young people's personal aspirations—rather than actual plans—towards marriage.

Overview

Marital aspirations

Table 1

Yes %	No %	Don't have a view %
70	18	12

As Table 1 shows, over two-thirds, 70 per cent, of the young people questioned think that they would like to get married one day. The findings reveal some differences between age groups, with younger people, for example, more likely to say that they would like to get married than the eldest cohort. Looking at sex, slightly more men than women have said yes to the question 'Would you like to get married one day?' but the difference is comparatively small. Where there is a significant difference is between the higher percentage of women who do *not* want to get married—as opposed to 'do not have a view'—compared to men.

Several questions arise through this initial finding, which can be addressed by looking at how respondents' answers break down according to demographic profiles.[†] As explained in the introduction, it is possible to determine how the responses break down according to respondents' ascribed characteristics and backgrounds. Throughout the write-up of the survey the choices of **main** reason cited for each question will be looked at by sex, age, relationship and parenting status and two approximate gauges of socio-economic class: education level determined by respondents' level of qualifications and social class category determined by occupation.[1] For the relevant sample as a whole, **all reasons** as well as main reasons are looked at.

[†] 'Demographic profile' here refers to age, sex, socio-economic status, relationship status and parenting status.

THE SURVEY: FINDINGS IN FULL

Who wants to get married?

Aspirations towards marriage according to demographic profiles

By sex and age

Looking at sex, a clear majority of both men and women would like to get married one day, although the percentage of men who want to marry is seven percentage points higher than that of women (74 percent compared to 67 per cent). The reason for this disparity between the sexes relates to the higher number of women who do not want to get married (whereas those not having a view accounted for only 11 per cent). Twenty-two per cent of women compared to 14 per cent of men in the survey say that they do not want to marry. The possible explanation for why this might be is discussed in 'Survey conclusions' (p. 151). In relation to age, the youngest age group, 20-24 year-olds, are most likely to want to get married one day with 76 percent saying 'yes' to the question, compared to 69 per cent of 25-29 year-olds and 64 per cent of 30-35 year-olds. The 12-percentage point gap between the youngest and eldest groups may relate to new perceptions of marriage, more 'idealism' amongst younger people and circumstances which rule marriage out amongst the older group. In line with this, 25 per cent of 30-35 year-olds, compared to 12 per cent of those respondents in the youngest category, do not want to marry. [Tables 2 and 3: Appendix 1]

By socio-economic class

There are strong associations between socio-economic class, as measured by the qualifications level of the respondent (their 'educational level') and social class category, and their aspirations towards marriage. Notably, those in the higher socio-economic classes are considerably more likely to want to get married one day: 75 per cent in the highest education level category, 1, and 78 per cent in the second highest, 2, compared to 51 per cent in the lowest, 4. Similarly, looking at social class category, there is a 26-percentage point gap between the highest category, AB, and the lowest, E. Those in social class category E are much more likely to say 'no' to wanting to marry (31 per cent compared to 10 per cent in category AB). Equally, those in the bottom two education levels are significantly more likely to say that they do not want to marry (34 per cent (4) and 21 per cent (3) compared to 11 per cent and 13 per cent in levels 2 and 1). [Tables 4 and 5: Appendix 1]

From the lower proportions of respondents wanting to get married and higher proportion not wanting to marry within the lower socio-economic categories, it is evident that, at least in this population, there is a relationship between social class and marital aspirations. The possible reasons behind this relationship between socio-economic status and aspirations towards marriage are discussed in detail in 'Survey conclusions', (p. 151).

By relationship and parenting status

Respondents' relationship and parenting status draws out further patterns. [Tables 6 and 7: Appendix 1]

By relationship status
Looking at relationship status, those respondents who are cohabiting are most likely to want to marry. 79 per cent of cohabiting respondents have said 'yes' to wanting to get married one day compared to 69 per cent of those respondents who are single and 33 per cent of those who are separated. That marriage is most popular amongst cohabiting respondents is likely to relate to the fact that they already have a partner whom they would like to marry. As is discussed in 'Survey conclusions' (p. 151), the popularity of marriage amongst people who are already in a live-in partnership indicates that there is a perceived difference between living together and getting married.

For single people, whom unsurprisingly the demographic data show to be disproportionately likely to be in the lowest age-range, perhaps the possibility of meeting the 'right' person in the future is likely to make marriage a future ideal. Respondents who are separated are least likely to aspire to marriage and most likely to *not* want to marry. This may relate to a less idealised perception of relationships on account of having experienced a separation, or indeed marriage. Whilst 18 per cent of single people and only 11 per cent of cohabiting respondents do not want to marry, a much higher 52 per cent of those who have separated have said 'no' in answer to whether they would like to get married one day.

By parenting status
In relation to parenting status, respondents without children are 12 percentage points more likely to want to marry than those who are parents; parents are also 12 percentage points more likely to say that

they would *not* like to marry than non-parents. This difference between parents and non-parents very likely relates to differing attitudes to parenting outside marriage. As the results below indicate, a popular reason for wanting to marry is so as to have children within marriage, a view which is less common, unsurprisingly, amongst unmarried parents. Shown through demographic cross-tabulation (see Appendix 2), there is in addition a relationship between parenting status and socio-economic class which may be relevant to aspirations towards marriage (again, discussed in Survey conclusions, p. 151).

2. Question: Here are some reasons people have given for getting married. Which of these, if any, do you think would apply to you?

Having gained an idea of whether unmarried people aspire to marriage, the next point of research has been to find out why those surveyed who *do* want to marry take this view—as well as why those already married decided to marry. This question has been asked to all 20-35 year-olds in the sample (including those who are already married and those who have said that they do not have a view) apart from those respondents who have said that they do not want to get married. Respondents have been asked to choose their main reason, out of a list of options, then their next two most important reasons. The main— 'most important'—reasons have been broken down according to respondents' demographic backgrounds.

Overview

Table 8, (p. 158) shows the reasons for wanting to get married listed according to their popularity as the main (most important) reason chosen for wanting to marry.

Main reason

As Table 8 shows, wanting to commit to one's partner is the most popular reason for wanting to get married. Commitment has been chosen as the most important reason by an average of 47 per cent of the cohort, and by slightly more women than men. A higher number of cohabiting respondents have chosen this reason than those with other relationship statuses. The popularity of commitment amongst cohabiting couples helps to explain why cohabiting people see marriage as different from living together, and therefore as an aspiration for the future.

Main reason for wanting to marry

Table 8

Reason	%
I want to commit to my partner	47
I want to bring up my children within marriage	15
None of these	8
For religious reasons	5
Family expectations	4
I think that being married makes for more emotional security	6
Because I want to respect traditional values	5
I think that being married makes for more financial security	4
It's important to my partner to be married	3
Other	2
Specific practical*	1

* Specific practical reason e.g. tax/immigration purposes

Age appears to make little difference to respondents' main reason for wanting to marry. Having children within marriage is the second most popular reason for wanting to marry. This option has been chosen as the main reason by 15 per cent of respondents, showing no significant differences by age or sex. Financial security, emotional security, importance to partner, religion, family expectations, traditional values and practical reasons have each been chosen by comparatively small numbers of respondents. 'None of these' has been chosen by the third highest number, eight per cent.

All reasons

As well as choosing a main reason, respondents could choose up to two more reasons for wanting to marry. The two answers which stand out, shown in Table 9 (p. 159), are again, commitment and having children within marriage, chosen by 58 per cent and 44 per cent respectively. There is a significant drop to the next most popular reasons: emotional security ranks third, chosen by 21 per cent and traditional values has been chosen by 16 per cent. Financial reasons (14 per cent), religious reasons (10 per cent) and the wishes of their partner (10 per cent) are the next most popular, with only two per cent saying that marriage is important to them for practical reasons.

All reasons for wanting to marry

Table 9

Reason	%
I want to commit to my partner	58
I want to bring up my children within marriage	44
I think that being married makes for more emotional security	21
Because I want to respect traditional values	16
I think that being married makes for more financial security	14
Family expectations	13
For religious reasons	10
It's important to my partner to be married	10
None of these	8
Other	4
Specific practical	2

Differences in priority according to demographic profile
By sex
When the data on the main reason for wanting to marry is broken down by sex, although broadly similar, there are some differences. Women are four percentage points more likely than men to choose commitment as their main reason for wanting to get married (49 per cent compared to 45 per cent). Women are also five percentage points more likely than men to choose wanting to raise children within marriage as their main reason for wanting to marry (17 per cent compared to 12 per cent). [Table 10: Appendix 1]

By age
When the data is broken down by age group, there are no notable differences. Across the age groups commitment is the most popular

main reason for wanting to marry, from 50 per cent amongst the youngest group to 46 and 47 per cent in the other two age groups. Having children within marriage is the second most popular, with a significant drop (between 14 and 16 per cent choosing this option as their main reason). [Table 11: Appendix 1]

By socio-economic class
Using social class category and education level, patterns between socio-economic groups can be gauged about the main reason for wanting to marry. Looking at reasons chosen for wanting to get married, the majority response is the same for each social class category and education level—commitment. The percentages vary, however, with commitment generally gaining more support higher up the socio-economic scale: for example, commitment is 13 percentage points more popular amongst the highest social class category, AB, than the lowest social class category, E (54 per cent compared to 41 per cent). Similarly commitment is 18 percentage points more popular amongst those in the highest education level, 1, than those in the lowest, 4 (52 per cent compared to 34 per cent). With a significant drop in percentage to around 15 per cent, wanting to have children within marriage is generally the second most common choice for wanting to get married— except for the lowest social class categories and the lowest education level. For the lowest education level 'none of these' is the second most popular, as it is for the lowest social class category. [Tables 12 and 13: Appendix 1]

By relationship status
Priorities for getting married are broadly similar across relationship statuses, in the sense that the primary reason for each wanting to get married is to commit to a partner. The levels of support for this option do however differ according to relationship status. Cohabiting respondents are the most likely to choose commitment (56 per cent) and separated respondents the least likely to choose commitment (31 per cent). The next most popular reason for all respondents, except separated ones, is wanting to bring up children within marriage, although the percentages drop down considerably, to 15 per cent (cohabiting respondents) and 16 per cent (married) and 19 per cent (single respondents). The second most popular reason for separated

THE SURVEY: FINDINGS IN FULL

people is 'none of these' (21 per cent), which by contrast is chosen by much smaller percentages of those in other relationship statuses (between five and 10 per cent). Other notable differences include a considerably lower number of cohabiting respondents choosing religion as a main reason for getting married (one per cent compared to between five and 10 per cent); family expectations is also less likely to be chosen by cohabiting respondents than the other relationship statuses. Separated respondents are more likely to choose 'other' and married respondents least likely (four per cent and one per cent respectively). [Table 14: Appendix 1]

By parenting status

The main reason for wanting to get married differs very little between parenting statuses, the three most popular main reasons being selected by the similar percentages. The most chosen main reason for wanting to marry is commitment, chosen by 46 and 48 per cent respectively. The second most popular choice for both is marrying to bring up children within marriage (15 and 14 per cent) and the third 'none of these' (eight per cent). [Table 15: Appendix 1]

3. **Question: You mentioned that you would like to bring up your children within marriage. Here are some reasons that other people have given for saying this. Which of these, if any, do you think would apply to you?**

In the pilot survey carried out in order to develop a comprehensive set of questions and response options, many respondents picked 'to have children' as a reason for wanting to get married. Consequently the decision was made to add a follow-on question in the survey, after reasons for wanting to marry, in order to understand why being married was important to people when they parented.

Wanting to marry (this question has been asked to married as well as unmarried respondents) in order to have children within marriage is the second most popular main reason and the second most popular reason overall (taken from 'all reasons', Table 9). Forty-four per cent of respondents have said that one of the reasons they want to get married is because they want to raise their children within marriage. This has been chosen as the main reason for wanting to get married by 15 per cent of respondents.

The aim of Question 3 is to understand the difference that respondents think marriage makes to raising children.

Overview

Main reason for wanting to have children within marriage
Stable environment is very popular across the board, chosen by 70 per of respondents and by even more amongst those who are already married. Tradition is the second most popular choice although it has received only 12 per cent support. Few respondents have chosen the alternative options and there are few differences by age, sex and parenting status. [Table 16: Appendix 1]

Table 16

Reasons	%
I think that being married is more likely to create a stable environment for children	70
I want a traditional family	12
I think that being married gives children more long-term financial security (including in the event of divorce)	8
I think it is more socially acceptable if children are brought up within marriage	6
None of these	3
Other	1

All reasons
Stable environment is still overwhelmingly the most popular reason chosen by 79 per cent of people, although the other options receive slightly more support when all options are taken into account. Wanting a traditional family is second most popular, chosen by 31 per cent of respondents, and financial security and social acceptability have been chosen by 22 per cent and 17 per cent respectively. There are few differences by age or sex. [Table 17: Appendix 1]

THE SURVEY: FINDINGS IN FULL

All reasons for wanting to have children within marriage

Table 17

Reason	%
I think that being married is more likely to create a stable environment for children	79
I want a traditional family	31
I think that being married gives children more long-term financial security (including in the event of divorce)	22
I think it is more socially acceptable if children are brought up within marriage	17
None of these	3
Other	1

Reasons for wanting to have children within marriage according to demographic profile

By sex

When the data is broken down by sex, there is very little difference between men and women. Both men and women therefore are most likely to choose stability (80 and 79 per cent), followed by a drop wanting a traditional family (30 and 32 per cent). [Table 18: Appendix 1]

By age

Looking at age, there are again only small differences between the three age groups, with stability and tradition still the first and second main choices. The only notable difference is between the youngest age group and the eldest age group's selection of marriage as providing financial security for children (23 per cent compared to 20 per cent). [Table 19: Appendix 1]

By relationship status

Marriage as the route to a stable environment for children is the most popular reason for wanting to have children within marriage across relationship statuses. Married people are however considerably more likely to choose this option than cohabiting couples (74 per cent compared to 61 per cent). [Table 20: Appendix 1]

By parenting status
The responses are largely very similar between parents and non-parents, with the exception of believing that marriage leads to more financial security for children. Respondents without children are twice as likely to choose this response than those with (ten per cent compared to five per cent). [Table 21: Appendix 1]

By socio-economic status
Respondents at each education level have chosen 'to create a stable environment' for children as the main reason for wanting to marry, although the support for this answer is lowest from the lowest education level, 1 (55 per cent). [Tables 22 and 23: Appendix 1]

Looking at social class category, a stable environment for children is once again the most popular main reason, with broadly similar levels of support (ranging from 75 per cent for social class AB to 68 per cent for social class CD). For AB, C2 and D the second most popular main response is giving children more long-term financial stability in the event of divorce: for social class categories C1 and E it is believing that having children within marriage is more socially acceptable.

4. Question: Here are some reasons people have given for not yet having decided to get married. Which of these, if any, do you think would apply to you?

This question has been asked of unmarried respondents who have expressed a desire to marry in the future. The aim of this question is to get an understanding of why respondents who want to marry have not yet done so—in other words, what preconditions, from age to financial circumstances, young people think are important when getting married.

Overview

Main reason
The most popular main reason for not yet having married is not yet having met the right person (29 per cent). By age group, the youngest group have shown that they like their freedom (18 per cent of 20-24 year-olds compared to five per cent of 30-35 year-olds), as do more men than women (22 per cent compared to 17 per cent). A significant number of respondents do not agree with any of the choices offered (13 per cent) and a moderate number say that getting married is not a

priority for them (nine per cent). Not being able to afford a wedding is a hurdle for a significant percentage of the sample (four per cent). All other choices have been selected by comparatively few respondents. [Table 24: Appendix 1]

Main reason for not yet having married

Table 24

Reason	%
I haven't yet met anyone I want to marry	29
I'm enjoying my current freedom	12
None of these	13
Getting married is not a high priority for me at the moment	9
I can't yet afford the wedding I want	6
I haven't been in my current relationship long enough	6
I'm waiting for my partner to propose	5
I am not currently in the financial position I would like to be in when I marry	4
My partner and I are not currently in a suitable financial position	4
I'm not sure I want to get married	4
Other	3
I'm not sure whether I want to marry my current partner	2
I haven't discussed marriage with my current partner	2
My partner doesn't want to get married	1
I'm waiting until I want to have children	-
Marriage is not currently available to same-sex couples	-

All reasons

The reason most frequently chosen is that people have not yet met the right person (31 per cent). The second most chosen response is that people are enjoying their freedom (19 per cent), especially with younger people (18 per cent of 20-24 year-olds compared to five per cent of 30-35 year-olds). The third most popular reason is that marriage is not a priority (16 per cent). Several choices have received a moderate level of response. A few respondents feel that they have not been in their current relationship long enough (nine per cent), and there is a small but notable group, composed mainly of women, who are waiting for their partner to propose to them (seven per cent). Financial matters are important to a moderate number in the sample, both in the immediate sense of not being able to afford their ideal wedding (ten per cent), and as a more general concern about financial security (seven per cent for personal finance and seven per cent for finance as a couple). The other options have received relatively little support. [Table 25: Appendix 1]

All reasons for not yet having married

Table 25

Reason	%
I haven't yet met anyone I want to marry	31
I'm enjoying my current freedom	19
Getting married is not a high priority for me at the moment	16
None of these	13
I can't yet afford the wedding I want	10
I haven't been in my current relationship long enough	9
I am not currently in the financial position I would like to be in when I marry	7
My partner and I are not currently in a suitable financial position	7
I'm waiting for my partner to propose	7
I'm waiting until I want to have children	1
I haven't discussed marriage with my current partner	4
Other	4
I'm not sure whether I want to marry my current partner	4
My partner doesn't want to get married	1
I'm not sure I want to get married	6
Marriage is not currently available to same-sex couples	1

Main reason for not yet having married according to demographic profile
By Sex

Looking at the reasons for waiting to get married broken down according to sex, there are broad similarities across the choices for men and women, however with three interesting differences. Whilst both men and women have chosen not having met the right person as their main reason for not yet having married, there is a difference between men and women's second most popular reason: men are most likely to say that they are enjoying their current freedom (22 per cent compared to 17 per cent women) and women are most likely to say 'marriage is not a high priority for me at the moment' (18 per cent compared to 15 per cent). The second, and perhaps related, difference is that nearly four times as many women as men have chosen 'waiting to be proposed to' as their main reason for not yet having married (11 per cent compared to three per cent). The third notable difference between the choices of men and women is that women are more than twice as likely (although the overall number is relatively small) to select 'my partner and I are not currently in a suitable financial position to marry' (eight per cent compared to five per cent of men). [Table 26: Appendix 1]

By age
Looking at the reasons for postponing marriage according to age group, there are several differences. Not having met anyone to marry is, across the age groups, the most popular main reason for not yet having married; this option has the greatest support from the eldest age group (37 per cent compared to 26 per cent). Enjoying their freedom is the second most popular main reason amongst only the youngest age group (18 per cent); amongst the other two older age groups the second most popular reason given is 'none of these' (13 per cent). The other responses have been chosen by broadly similar (small) proportions. [Table 27: Appendix 1]

By parenting status
Looking at the main reason for having postponed marriage by parenting status, not having met the right person is the most popular choice both amongst those with children and those without (22 per cent and 31 per cent respectively). For those who are not parents, the second most popular answer is enjoying their freedom (14 per cent), a response chosen by fewer than half the number of parents. For those respondents with children the second most popular response is not being able to afford the wedding that they want (14 per cent), an option much less popular amongst non-parents (four per cent). [Table 28: Appendix 1]

By relationship status

The main reason for not yet having married varies between relationship statuses. For single and separated people the most common reason is not having met the right person (38 per cent for both). Amongst cohabiting and single respondents, 'none of these' is much less popular, chosen by 15 per cent and 11 per cent respectively, compared to having been chosen by 23 per cent of separated people. Only a small proportion, seven per cent, of cohabiting respondents have chosen not having met the right person as their main reason for postponing marriage. For cohabiting people, the most popular main reason is 'none of these', chosen by 15 per cent of this population. The other two most popular options for cohabiting couples are practical reasons: not being able to afford the wedding they want, the second most common main reason (14 per cent), and not being in a suitable financial position (eight per cent). These two options are chosen by comparatively few amongst those of other relationship statuses: three per cent of single and no separated people have chosen the cost of the wedding as their main reason for postponing marriage, and one per cent and three per cent respectively of single and separated respondents have chosen 'my partner and I are not currently in a suitable financial position'. Cohabiting couples are also considerably more likely to choose not being in the financial position they want to be in than the other categories (eight per cent compared to two per cent and three per cent). Looking at the other main reasons for postponing marriage amongst single people, 'I am enjoying my current freedom' is the second most popular choice (15 per cent); this option has been chosen by considerably more single people than those in other categories (15 per cent compared to five per cent of cohabiting respondents and two per cent of separated respondents). [Table 29: Appendix 1]

By socio-economic class

All five social class categories have chosen not having met the right person as the most popular reason for not wanting to marry and at comparatively similar rates: between 27 per cent and 31 per cent. For social class categories AB, C1 and E, the second most popular reason for not having married is enjoying their current freedom (between 17 per cent (AB) and 12 per cent (C1 and E); for class C2 and D the second most popular main reason is 'none of these' (11 per cent and 18 per cent), an option which has comparatively high levels of support from the other social classes, although less from the lowest social class, E. The highest social class, AB, are the least likely to choose not being able to afford a wedding (four per cent), an option chosen most by social class category D and C2, and no respondents in social class category AB have chosen that they are not sure they want to get married as their reason for waiting to marry. 'Other', by contrast has been disproportionately picked by respondents in the highest social class category, AB (eight per cent compared to two, three, one and three per cent). [Tables 30 and 31: Appendix 1]

The most popular reason for not yet having married is the same across education levels, not having met the right person, chosen by between 27 and 30 per cent of respondents in each group. The second most popular reason, however, differs between education levels. For education levels 1, 3 and 4 'none of these' is second most popular (14, 14 and 13 per cent respectively); for education level 2, by contrast, the second most chosen reason is enjoying their freedom (15 per cent); this option has been chosen by fairly high numbers amongst those of education levels 1 and 3 (both 11 per cent), but fewer amongst those of education level 4 (seven per cent).

5 **Question: Here are some reasons people have given for not wanting to get married. Which of these, if any, do you think would apply to you?**

The aim of this question, which has been asked to all those respondents who have said that they would not like to marry, has been to explore their reasons for not wanting to get married.

It is important to note that the number of respondents in the sample answering this question is very small, 200. For analysis purposes this is significant as the smaller the size of the sample the less scope there is for it to be representative. The small size of the sample also means that a valid sub-categorisation of the answers is not possible.

Overview

Main reason for not wanting to marry

The most popular main reason for not wanting to marry is being happy in the situation that respondents are currently in (29 per cent). The next most popular main answer is thinking that marriage does not change a relationship (chosen by 15 per cent of respondents). Of the remaining choices most support is received by people saying that they are able to commit without marriage (chosen by eight per cent) and that marriage is outdated (chosen by seven per cent). There are a significant number who either do not agree with any of the reasons given or have other reasons ('other' and 'none of these', with a total of 13 per cent); all the other categories have been chosen by very small percentages.

Table 32

Reason	**(%)**
I am happy in my current situation	29
I don't think that marriage changes a relationship	15
None of these	8
My partner and I are committed to each other without getting married	8
I think marriage is outdated	7
Other	5
I want to avoid the financial responsibilities of divorce	5
I think that marriage is bad for equality between men and women	4
Fear of divorce	3
I would rather not enter into a legal and financial commitment	3
Marriage is not currently available to same-sex couples	3
I don't want to spend money on a wedding	2
I don't want to commit to one person	3
My parents were/are unhappily married	2
I think marriage is for people who want to have children	1
Don't know	1
My partner doesn't want to get married	*

* Chosen by too few to be eligible for significance testing

THE SURVEY: FINDINGS IN FULL

All reasons for not wanting to marry

Table 33

Reason	%
I am happy in my current situation	43
I don't think that marriage changes a relationship	27
I think marriage is outdated	17
My partner and I are committed to each other without getting married	16
I want to avoid the financial responsibilities of divorce	10
I don't want to spend money on a wedding	9
Fear of divorce	8
I don't want to commit to one person	9
Other	8
None of these	8
I would rather not enter into a legal and financial commitment	7
My parents were/are unhappily married	7
I think that marriage is bad for equality between men and women	4
Marriage is not currently available to same-sex couples	3
I think marriage is for people who want to have children	4
My partner doesn't want to get married	2
Don't know	1

All reasons

Looking at all chosen answers, there is strong support for 'I am happy in my current situation', with nearly half of all respondents choosing it (43 per cent). The second most popular choice is thinking that marriage does not change a relationship, chosen as one of their answers by 27 per cent of the population. Unlike with main reasons, the third most common choice is 'I think that marriage is outdated', chosen by 17 per cent of the 200 respondents in this sample.

6. Question: Do you strongly agree, agree, neither agree nor disagree, strongly disagree or can't choose with the following statement: 'People who want children ought to get married'

This question, a replica from the 2002 British Social Attitudes Survey, has been asked to all respondents in the population. What is important about this question is that it involves the respondent making generalisations about marriage—as distinct from expressing personal aspirations such as in Questions 1-5.

Overview

Response to the statement 'People who want children ought to get married'

Table 34

Strongly agree %	Agree %	Neither agree nor disagree %	Disagree %	Strongly disagree %	Can't choose %
15	25	19	27	12	2

Aggregate of agree/disagree

Table 35

Agree %	Disagree %
40	39

Aggregate of agree/disagree amongst those who would like to marry in order to have children within marriage

Table 36

Agree %	Disagree %
30	29

THE SURVEY: FINDINGS IN FULL

Response according to marital aspiration (unmarrieds)

Table 37

	Strongly agree %	Agree %	Neither agree nor disagree %	Disagree %	Strongly disagree %	Can't choose %
Yes	14	27	19	27	12	2
No	5	14	16	36	29	2
Don't have a view	9	15	26	32	14	4

Aggregate agree/disagree according to marital aspiration (unmarrieds)

Table 38

	Agree %	Disagree %
Yes	41	39
No	19	64
Don't have a view	24	46

Opinion on whether people ought to be married when they have children is divided fairly equally. Approximately the same percentage agree and disagree with this statement, however there are significant differences between the two groups. Those who agree are more likely to want to marry one day (41 per cent of those who want to get married compared to 19 per cent of those who do not). Another interesting comparison is looking at the views of those who want to marry in order to have children on whether people with children ought to get married. Table 36 shows that 30 per cent agreed with the statement and 29 per cent disagreed.

Response to the statement that people who want children ought to get married according to demographic profile

By sex
Women are less likely than men to agree with the statement (37 per cent compared to 43 per cent), with 35 per cent of women compared to 43 per cent of men disagreeing. [Table 39: Appendix 1]

By age
Looking at response according to age, there is virtually no difference at all between age groups, with around 39 per cent agreeing and 39 per disagreeing across the board. [Table 40: Appendix 1]

By socio-economic status
Respondents in all but the lowest social class category, E, show similar response rates; between 40 and 42 per cent agree with the statement that people who have children ought to marry, and between 36 per cent and 41 per cent disagree. Only 28 per cent of respondents in class E, by contrast, agree, and 53 per cent disagree. [Tables 41 and 42: Appendix 1]

Respondents amongst education levels 2 to 4 are more likely to disagree with the statement than agree with it, with a high of 44 per cent disagreeing in the lowest education level, level 4. Those people with the highest level of education, level 1, are more likely to agree with the statement than disagree with it (44 per cent agreeing).

By relationship status
Married respondents are the only relationship status to be more likely to agree with the statement than disagree with it; the greatest difference is between married and cohabiting people, where 50 per cent of married people agree that people who want children ought to marry, compared to 27 per cent of those cohabiting. Similarly, whilst 28 per cent of married people disagree with the statement, 52 per cent of cohabiting people disagree. [Table 43: Appendix 1]

By parenting status
Parents are more likely to disagree with the statement that people who want children ought to get married, whereas non-parents are more likely to agree. 42 per cent of those without children, compared to 37 per cent of those with children, agreed with the statement. In line with this, 44 per cent of parents disagreed with the statement compared to 36 per cent of non-parents. [Table 44: Appendix 1 shows]

7. Question: Do you strongly agree, agree, neither agree nor disagree, strongly disagree or can't choose with the following statement: 'Married people are generally happier than unmarried people'

THE SURVEY: FINDINGS IN FULL

As with Question 6, this question is a replica from the 2002 British Social Attitudes Survey. The aim again has been to gauge whether there is a disparity between whether respondents would like to get married and whether they believe that married people generally are happier.

This question has been asked of all respondents.

Overview

Response to the question 'Married people are generally happier than unmarried people'

Table 45

Strongly agree	Agree	Neither agree nor disagree	Disagree	Strongly disagree	Can't choose
%	%	%	%	%	%
8	17	28	29	14	4

Aggregate of agree/disagree

Table 46

Agree	Disagree
%	%
25	43

Response according to marital aspiration (unmarrieds)

Table 47

	Strongly agree	Agree	Neither agree nor disagree	Dis-agree	Strongly disagree	Can't choose
	%	%	%	%	%	%
Yes	6	14	29	34	14	3
No	1	4	21	42	30	3
Don't have a view	4	11	28	29	20	8

Overall, significantly more people disagree with this statement and a very high percentage of respondents neither agree nor disagree (28 per cent). Of those that want to marry one day 20 per cent think that married people generally are happier and 48 per cent disagree with the statement. Those who do not want to marry show the strongest belief that married people are not happier (72 per cent).

Aggregate agree/disagree according to marital aspiration (unmarrieds)

Table 48

	Agree %	Disagree %
Yes	20	48
No	4	72
Don't have a view	15	49

Response to the statement that married people are generally happier than unmarried people according to demographic profile

By sex
Women are significantly more likely to disagree than agree with the statement, with 48 per cent disagreeing and only 21 per cent agreeing. Men are also more likely to not think that married people are happier, with 38 per cent disagreeing with the statement and 29 per cent agreeing. [Table 49: Appendix 1]

By age
Respondents in all three age groups are more likely to disagree than agree with the statement that married people are happier. Those in the youngest category, 20-24, are most likely to disagree (50 per cent) and the number agreeing in this age group is only 18 per cent. [Table 50: Appendix 1]

By socio-economic status
Across social class category, respondents are more likely to disagree than agree with the statement. Those in the lowest social class category, E, are 12 percentage points more likely to disagree with the statement than those in the highest social class category, AB (52 per cent compared to 40 per cent). [Tables 51 and 52: Appendix 1]

Across education levels respondents are more likely to disagree than agree with the statement that married people are happier. Whilst around 24 to 25 per cent of respondents agree with the statement across education levels, the number of people disagreeing with the statement is significantly lower for those respondents in education level 1 (35 per cent compared to 50 per cent in level 4).

By relationship status

Married respondents are most likely to agree that married people are happier (42 per cent) and cohabiting respondents least likely to agree (12 per cent). Those cohabiting are also most likely to disagree with the statement (59 per cent), followed by separated people (52 per cent). [Table 53: Appendix 1]

By parenting status

There is very little difference between the views of respondents when they are sorted according to whether they have children or not. Both parents and non-parents are more likely to disagree with the statement that married people are happier (38 and 48 per cent), with only 27 and 23 per cent respectively, agreeing. [Table 54: Appendix 1]

Conclusion

Family policy is currently politically divided. The focus of the Conservative Party is to foster the two-parent, self-reliant family. As the term conservatism suggests, shifts away from the nuclear family, over the past 50 years in particular, are perceived as having had a negative effect on society: breaking down private systems of mutual support and undermining personal responsibility. Put crudely, rising divorce rates, sinking levels of marriage and increases in the number of single parents are perceived to signal disappearing family values and the root of our social problems. In policy terms for the Conservative Party, support for the two-parent family has meant promoting marriage in order to stabilise partnerships (in part by making them legally binding) and asserting the responsibility of fathers, both for the purposes of providing role models and also to avoid mother-and-child financial dependence on the state. A recent addendum to their central family policies under Cameron, the Conservatives have sought to focus increased attention on facilitating childcare for working parents.

By contrast, New Labour's focus is to allow for family diversity—not to give preference to one form over another. Child welfare is a key priority (with child welfare primarily associated with household income), as is women's right to work, with emphasis on facilitating the combination of work and childcare. Rising divorce rates, sinking levels of marriage and increases in the number of single parents are more likely to be interpreted as outcomes of disappearing oppressive norms and the democratisation of family life than as problematic to either individual or society. In policy terms for the New Labour government, the approach has been to focus on increasing family income (particularly amongst those families on lower levels), employment legislation to accommodate childcare and public subsidy of formal childcare provision.

The contrast between the views of the interviewees who are associated either with the Left or a neutral position, and those associated with the Right or a 'traditional' position, mirror this party-political dichotomy. Therefore, the conclusion might well be that there *is* a grassroots political divide on the family which politicians are simply articulating through their policies. All importantly however, the division which does exist is not a fundamental one. There may not be an ideological consensus, but there can and needs to be consensual practical policy which moves on from political positioning.

The interviews highlight that family 'values' are broadly similar across the political and ideological spectrum. The survey highlights the common value attached to committed unions amongst Britain's young people in parallel with a liberalism towards *other people's* family relationships. This challenges the current party-political climate which has pitted 'tradition' against 'progressiveness'. Embracing diversity and not judging between alternative family structures need not equate with a rejection of the so-called traditional—married, two-parent—family. Equality between the sexes in relationships, as well as new opportunities to end them if they do not work out, has helped reconcile the 'traditional' family structure with the ideals of modern liberalism. Case in point, in the context of parenting, polling shows a concurrent importance attached to marriage *and* divorce amongst the British public.[1] Seemingly counter-intuitively, the availability of divorce has arguably elevated the value of marriage in the sense that marriages today can more often be taken to represent successful partnerships—as opposed to simply representing the past normative pressures against ending them. Civil partnerships and new reproductive technologies, furthermore, mean that two-parent families and legally recognised committed unions have been updated to make them universally available.

Politicians' rhetoric continues to give the impression that Left and Right are fundamentally at odds with each other when it comes to family values. However there is little to support this idea at a grassroots level. If those associated with the Left believed, for example, that the two-parent family was inherently negative, perhaps because of associations with the normative pressures of the past, then priorities and goals between Left and Right would be fundamentally at odds. This might arguably have been the case for some sections of the Left during the disestablishmentarianism of Second Wave feminism. However, as the interviews and survey illustrate, today this does not appear to be so. Shared responsibility between parents, and stability come at the top of most people's agenda for the family; committed relationships are perceived as valuable for adults and children alike, and parental separation as difficult. There are considerable differences in emphasis and level of nuance, especially in relation to when couple parenting does not work out, but the *ideals* appear to be very similar across the ideological spectrum.

The key family policy priorities of the Left—the pursuit of equality across class, gender and household, a better work/childcare balance for mothers—fit neatly within the Right's pursuit of enforcing paternal responsibility and personal responsibility. Similarly, the Left's focus on tackling child poverty is intrinsic to addressing what conservatives refer to as 'family breakdown'. The compatibility of Left and Right key priorities, together with identifiable shared family ideals from the survey and interviews, demonstrate that a consensual family policy is both a realistic ambition and a necessary one.

What is needed to achieve a unified set of policies is a re-conceptualisation of the boundaries between ideology and practical policy-making. Common family policy goals are attainable across political divides despite there being ideological differences. Whether the intention behind policy aiming to drive home paternal responsibility, for example, is to foster greater gender equality or to provide children with male role models, does not matter. The ultimate aim is the same: fathers' involvement.

There is currently a polarisation between Left and Right in the *policy approach* they are prepared to take. The Labour government and the Left more generally are hugely resistant to getting involved in the subject of family structure, for fear of being prescriptive. They opt instead to focus on what they see as supporting those families which need supporting the most. The Conservatives and the Right more generally strive to influence behaviour in order to produce the family outcomes they see as preferable. In other words, the Left sees the role of government as being to intervene only in outcomes, the Right to promote particular structures. With children at the heart of the political imagination concerning family policy today, both Labour and the Conservatives argue that their order of priorities puts children first: Labour by helping all families regardless of the choices that parents make, the Conservatives by promoting the structure which they consider best for children—the married family. More satisfactory would be a balance between these two approaches which provides immediate support for all families, and thereby all children as well as all parents, whilst making policy for the longer-term which recognises positive situations and aspirations and strives to foster them.

CONCLUSION

In conclusion successful family policy needs to circumvent both New Labour's avoidance of the significance of parenting structure on the basis of its associations with prescription, and the Conservatives' over-attachment to structure for structure's sake. By sticking to this stubborn dichotomy, neither party can make satisfactory family policy. Left and Right need to borrow from each other. The Conservatives' family policy-making currently lacks the wide lens; New Labour's family policy-making currently lacks a long lens; effective family policy requires both.

Towards a consensual family policy

Labour wants to increase life chances amongst children, foster gender equality, reduce poverty and create greater social equality. The Conservatives prioritise stable families, rewarding commitment and minimising the numbers of people on social assistance, thus preventing what they perceive to be the outcomes of broken families (crime and drug and alcohol abuse, for example). The similarities between the two sets of goals need recognition. Parental separation is both a generator and *outcome* of poverty, it jeopardises the possibility of parenting equality, and it makes combining work and childcare much more difficult for women in particular.

Whilst the aim of New Labour family policy is to embrace diversity and change, their position on family policy is ironically narrow-minded. The fact that parental separation is greatly undermining the left-wing agenda ought to make parenting structure a primary interest of the Left. Yet Labour considers an interest in family structure to be Conservative moralising territory. A reactive stance *vis-à-vis* Conservative policy is the government's Achilles' heel on the family. Marriage provides a pertinent example. Labour sees supporting marriage as doable only along Conservative Party lines. Not wanting to privilege it as the Conservatives have proposed has therefore led to withdrawing virtually all support, practical and rhetorical, for marriage. As such Alan Johnson speaking as Education Secretary in 2007 concurrently argued that strong relationships were the key to successful parenting, and marriage the pinnacle of a strong relationship, but, essentially, that marriage was an irrelevance to government policy.[2] This was a notable departure from New Labour's 1998 declaration in the Green Paper *Supporting Families* that '…it makes sense for the Government to do what it can to strengthen marriage'.[3]

Similarly, the Labour government has shied away from supporting —as well as talking about—the two-parent family for fear that it might be interpreted as criticism of other forms of family. As such, Prime Minister Tony Blair's 'conservatism' on the family was treated by many in the Labour Party as a foible best kept at bay.

The importance of attaching no importance to family structure has become central to discussion about family on the Left. The rationale behind this is understandable. Under the last Conservative administrations, the married two-parent family was presented as the only truly legitimate family form. The portrayal of the 'optimal' nuclear family, with its two opposite-sex married parents, was exclusive: to homosexuals, to cohabiting parents, to those for whom couple parenting had not worked out. In defence of those disqualified, the liberal reaction has been to condemn this exclusivity and to concentrate on celebrating diversity in family structure. The problem today is that the current government is effectively repeating the same mutually exclusive stance—we cannot support two-parent families and alternatives simultaneously—for which they have deliberately positioned themselves in opposition to the Conservatives. Added to this, Labour's attitude is that in any case little could be done to influence family structure even were it desirable: people will live their lives the way they want no matter what government does. This perspective goes back to a focus on autonomous choice—a naïve position, discussed further below, which fails to differentiate active choice from the impact of circumstance on family patterns. New Labour's position on this also relates to past—Conservative—governments' failed attempts to affect family structure: once again, a highly reactive stance.

Liberal Democrat children's spokesperson Annette Brooke argues that the Conservatives are perceived to have a 'monopoly' on family policy; the reactive stance of left-wing politics has allowed this to happen. New Labour must define its family policies in line with its own priorities—rather than simply opposing Conservative policy.

Family structure *does* matter—but in much less simplistic terms than the Conservative championing of the intact two-parent family suggests. In terms of the responsibility of co-parenting, structure is highly relevant right across family types: from same-sex adopted families to single-parent families, because in the majority of cases parenting started out as a partnership. As such there is no need for the Left to avoid the issue for fear of being judgemental.

Ultimately the aim of family policy should be to foster stability. Stability is achieved through well-functioning arrangements regarding work, childcare and the interface, continuity for children, the fulfilment of parental responsibilities and thereby parenting equality. Instability in family life both denotes and leads to difficulties for children and parents. Working to achieve stable families does not mean forcing dysfunctional families to stay together; on the contrary it means fostering parenting partnerships which work and lead to the best outcomes for children, and ensuring continuity in the event of parental separation. Making it more difficult for parents to separate should not be the aim; rather the aim should be to make it *easier to stay together*. Similarly stability does not necessitate convention: 'new' family forms, such as same-sex partnerships, can be equally stable. There is a significant difference between diversity and instability; however policymakers are not satisfactorily delineating them.

Labour is currently resistant to discussing the prevention of parental separation. Doing so is perceived as problematising parental separation, which is interpreted as its *condemnation*. This narrow reading imposes unnecessary, as well as illogical, limits on the government's family policy. The purpose of problematising parental separation needs to be re-conceptualised by New Labour. The aim should be to look at the bigger picture and the longer-term, adding a complementary *pro*active dimension to their current *re*active approach. At present the Labour government concentrates on dealing with the outcomes of parental separation. A more ambitious strategy would be to focus on addressing the causes of parental separation *as well as* dealing with the outcomes. With couple-parenting deemed preferable by most parents and the pain of separation very difficult for many, as evidenced in the interviews, addressing the causes would help parents fulfil their aspirations, as well as helping to mitigate their difficulties. Doing so would be neither reactionary nor prescriptive, two of Labour—and the Left's more generally—main fears. So how can policy foster family stability? How can policy be proactive without being prescriptive? The most effective way is to identify the factors which lead to family *in*stability.

The Conservative point of view is that the greatest source of family instability is non-marriage. Consequently, their strategy is to champion marriage by showing that statistically speaking marriages last longer than other forms of partnership and thereby create a more stable environment for children. The Conservative Party therefore takes the line that in the interests of stability, promoting marriage should be at the centre of family policy. The problem with this position is that, as many of the interviewees have argued, the equation is less straightforward: the Conservatives are conflating correlation with causality. What generally creates the comparative longevity of marriage today is the mutual commitment of the marrying couple, rather than just the act of marrying. In other words, marriage today tends to be a signpost for, rather than a generator of, commitment. Simply getting all unmarried couples to legalise their relationship would therefore not produce the stability associated with marriage.

Nevertheless, although the Conservative's analysis of marriage is flawed, they are right in saying that for parents non-marriage can be a sign of instability. As sociologists Kathleen Kiernan and Kate Pickett put it:

> The absence of the legal bond of marriage among cohabiting couples may represent less economic or emotional security, which may lie behind the higher dissolution rate invariably found among cohabiting couples.[4]

As mentioned earlier in relation to the survey, there is extensive evidence that parents in poorer socio-economic groups are less likely to marry. The detail of the research finds that this does not result from a disinterest in marriage but from the fact that the commitment associated with marriage is perceived both to be less available and to be 'riskier'. One of the primary reasons that low-income women, for example, are reluctant to commit relates to the poor employment profiles and economic prospects of their pool of potential husbands. In the current British context there is the added possibility that the low/no-income partner may even be an economic drain in cases where having a partner conflicts with social assistance entitlements for low-income parents.

The comparative longevity of marriage today (children with unmarried parents are nearly twice as likely to see their parents split up before their sixteenth birthday than those with married parents, for example)[5] is often dismissed as a 'selection' effect. As several of the interviewees have argued, marriages last longer because of the *type* of people who marry: in other words, the sort of people who are 'selected into' marriage. Yet this really is the point rather than the caveat. The better-educated and better-off financially are more likely to get married and stay married. This indicates that marriage is a luxury good; it is not that the more affluent have different values but that they have circumstances more likely to attain them. For this reason it is fundamentally important that policymakers do not simply dismiss the disparity between married and unmarried parents but rather seek to understand what factors might be thwarting the achievability of contexts conducive to marriage. With economics playing such a significant role in UK marital patterns, Harriet Harman is misguided in perceiving marriage to have 'no policy bite'.

As well as being less likely to marry, poor parents are more likely to separate and more likely to become single parents. With this strong correlation it is surprising that, given New Labour's concern about social exclusion, it disregards parental separation—and non-marriage—as a manifestation of deprivation. It does not even make political sense in light of the fact that the greatest proliferation of parental separation and unmarried parenthood in Britain occurred during the strains of high unemployment in the 1980s and early 1990s under the Conservatives. This exemplifies both the fact that unemployment and poverty can pull families apart and that Labour should be seizing the opportunity to 'reclaim' family structure from its current status as a Conservative hostage.

Nevertheless, the Labour position is that government should not take an interest in family structure but rather deal with outcomes. Labour is concerned about the poverty suffered by women and children as a result of parental separation—hence, for example, their New Deal for Lone Parents and child poverty targets—but *not* about the situations which may have led to their poverty. The problem is that by disregarding the implications of family structure Labour is allowing adversity for children and parents to go unaddressed. Family structure *is*, in other words, very much a part of the 'pragmatics' which Harriet Harman refers to, in light of the very practical effects of poverty on families; yet New Labour regards it solely as the domain of Conservative ideology. Polly Toynbee rightly argues that the conservative moralising agenda does not recognise that parental separation is often the better solution for mothers when men are a financial drain. However, both Right *and* Left do not sufficiently recognise that poverty—as opposed to straightforward choice—can cause parental break-up.

Parenting partnerships today do, of course, also face other strains relating not to practical elements, but to personal relations. A redefinition of partnerships and relationships has given more emphasis to emotional fulfilment. As a result relationships have become more 'high stakes' and therefore less stable. In some respects these higher expectations can be a mixed blessing. While new freedoms to experiment and leave relationships are positive, high expectations can become unrealistic expectations and fulfilment thereby less attainable. This is particularly so as notions of what constitutes emotional fulfilment are often heavily influenced by idealisations in the media.

The drawbacks of modern relationships really take effect when children are brought into the equation. Children make parents more mutually dependent than is the case for childless couples. Women's earning power today, for example, has enabled an independence in relationships without children, which does not apply as readily when children are involved. Although the importance of parents' happiness, both for their own lives and for the wellbeing of their children, should never be underestimated, notions of instant gratification for example, have undoubtedly put a burden on relationships which may well lead to greater unhappiness in the long-run.

There is, nevertheless, little that policy can—and arguably should—do to impact on relationship quality. The wider availability of counselling services for couples is certainly always welcome, however the scope that this type of provision can have is likely to be limited. Policy's relative powerlessness regarding the 'private' causes of parental separation re-emphasises the need for government to concentrate on the practical elements. The first is a focus on fostering functional families by addressing the issues causing instability. The second is ensuring that in the event of parental separation the family unit, in terms of dual responsibility between mothers and fathers, is maintained. One of the main reasons that the children of separated parents are more prone to face difficulties is because the two-parent structure in terms of responsibility—the 'dual-parenting'—collapses.

For the Left, in particular, one of the most compelling arguments for emphasising the significance of family structure is to ensure the equal participation of the non-resident parent in the event of parental separation. In the majority of cases the father is the non-resident parent; therefore if he is treated by policy as an 'optional extra' during the *intact* parenting relationship, the hope of a satisfactory co-parenting model after separation is heavily undermined. Even more importantly, there is currently a very narrow—*conservative*—conceptualisation on the Left of what is meant by attaching an importance to family structure and the two-parent family. Structure ought to refer as much to the parenting model as to the relationship between parents. For this reason it would be useful to stop talking about family breakdown and start talking about parental separation—and single parenting instead of lone parenting. The household may split, but the family unit—the parenting structure—should remain intact. As such mediation within divorce procedure (see Policy Recommendations) is as important for securing arrangements to maintain co-parenting post-separation, as it is to foster opportunities for reconciliation.

So how can the family unit be maintained post-separation? There are often practical obstacles around maintaining paternal responsibility after parents split. Financial contribution is frequently one of them. The non-resident father may not be able to afford to spend on a child he does not live with. However, even if the contribution is very low where, for example, the father's sole income is a low rate of social assistance, it is vital that the principle of financial responsibility is enforced. The same principle applies to fathers with additional families.

Such stipulations may sound draconian, particularly in cases where non-resident fathers argue that they 'wanted sex not a baby'. Yet what appears draconian may in fact be universally beneficial. Research at the University of Washington[6] has found that strict child maintenance laws lead to a decrease in the number of irresponsible fathers: men in states where paternal responsibility is strictly enforced are shown to be both more likely to use contraception and to support their children financially. Currently in the UK approximately only a third of parents *whose cases are registered* with the Child Support Agency, receive *any* maintenance at all from the non-resident parent.[7]

Much more satisfactory, however, is a relationship between non-resident father and child which goes beyond the financial. Research for the Joseph Rowntree Foundation has found that '...the most important thing for children was the extent to which both parents remained emotionally and practically committed to them after divorce or separation'.[8] Interviewee developmental psychologist Michael Lamb similarly argues that it is vital that the absent parent remains very much involved in a child's life—particularly in the mundane aspects, so that a long-lasting rather than a fragile 'weekend-dad' bond is established. However, as Duncan Fisher of the Fatherhood Institute points out, current child maintenance arrangements in this country work only on the basis of financial contribution.

Problems around non-resident father/child contact which relate to the mother's behaviour need also to be recognised. 'Bargaining' for time with the child in exchange for child maintenance is one way in which the resident parent may take control of the situation—and the child in the process. In some cases this may be the only way to get money out of the non-resident parent, but it is clearly not satisfactory. This scenario pleads the case for making child maintenance a formal arrangement, rather than an informal arrangement vulnerable to power struggles on top of irresponsibility, as is currently being proposed by the government.

Fiscally, New Labour has focused its support on single-parent families. While the urgent issue of poverty concentrated in single-parent households makes this an understandable focus, a broader strategy would be more effective in achieving the government's aims. In order to address the root of single parenting—parental separation—policy needs to also support other family structures. At the moment, government is not doing so either in the long-term or through social assistance arrangements. As several of the interviewees have argued (Liberal Democrat Annette Brooke, for example), low-income two-parent families are currently penalised in comparison to single-parent families—albeit inadvertently—much in the same way that unmarried couples would be were a married couples' allowance introduced. This is something which Labour has made a point of denouncing because it penalises children on the basis of their parents' actions. The problematic effect of current social assistance for families is that it further undermines the stability of low-income two-parent families. In the long run this may compound the risk of parental separation incurring the 'structural poverty' associated with single parenting. This issue needs to be addressed not by making single parents worse-off, but by better supporting two-parent families.

The emphasis on supporting single-parent families relates to the New Labour government's child poverty targets. If the government is to realise their aim of eradicating child poverty then they need to also address parental separation, thereby taking family structure into consideration. The danger is that in the run-up to missing the 2010 child poverty target the government will concentrate only on short-term solutions rather than seeking to address the root causes of family poverty. A one-pronged strategy to mitigate child poverty through social assistance is leaving the root causes unaddressed. Liberal Democrat Annette Brooke talks of the Labour and Liberal Democrat family policy approach as being a focus on children rather than the relationship between adults. However there is a distinction between the adult relationship and the *parenting relationship between adults* which left-wing politics is failing to recognise. Effective strategies to combat child poverty cannot treat children as detached from their parents.

Young people on low or no earned income are disproportionately likely to have children whose chances of their parents separating—and related, of poverty—are much higher. A longer term strategy for tackling child poverty therefore, run in parallel with short-term approaches, would be to introduce policies directed at those young men and women who are *most likely to be poor*.

To conclude, concrete policies such as raising employment amongst young people through welfare reforms and more effective vocational routes in schools are needed to foster stable and functional families. However, until an acknowledgement that family structure in terms of *support* matters, family policy will continue to be directionless.

Policy Recommendations

Key policy: tackling the route to family poverty
Identifying and tackling the roots of 'structural' poverty

The teaching of literacy and numeracy, reading in particular, continues to be highly problematic in primary schools. Over-regulation of teaching methods and curricula which thwart teacher responsiveness to pupils, and related issues with so-called 'teaching to the test' (cramming) in order to reach centralised targets, have led to a high number of pupils leaving primary school without a solid foundation in the basics. Once in secondary school, pupils lacking this vital foundation are not able to satisfactorily access the curriculum. Oversized school and class sizes exacerbate the situation by disabling teachers from identifying struggling pupils. Compounding this is the fact that the government's preferred route is academic (connected to a somewhat arbitrary drive to bolster graduate numbers), thereby undermining already weak vocational education provision. The net result of these difficulties is that a large number of 16-year-olds are leaving school with no qualifications and often no work prospects.

Added to this, today's unemployment arrangements mean that there is opportunity—albeit unintended—for continuous welfare reliance. As well as leading to stagnant dependency, this means that school leavers are presented with a financial pathway which requires neither qualifications nor labour.

Inadequate educational provision, together with the possibility of long-term welfare dependency, have led to a high number of young people 'not in education, employment or training'—NEETs—which has risen despite ten years of New Labour interventions. Almost a fifth of young people in England, Scotland and Wales are currently not in education, training or employment.[1] The effect on families is an increased risk that young women enter into parenthood in unstable circumstances, both financial and relational, in order to find a 'role' in life. One of the main difficulties with this is that it can lead both to poverty and long-term social assistance dependency. Connected to this are paternal circumstances. In areas where there is high unemployment and related deprivation, women are more likely to have less stable relationships with fathers who are out of work. This is related to the initial circumstances and timing of pregnancy, the strains of poverty on relationships and the potential impact of fathers who are not able to make sufficient financial contribution.

In other words, both female and male unemployment are strongly connected with family instability. A decline in *general* unemployment has perhaps been a distraction from the hugely problematic rise of worklessness amongst 16-24 year-olds. However it is the lack of occupation within this age group in particular which is setting parents and children off to an unstable start. In order to address this, the failings within primary and secondary education, particularly weak literacy skills and poor vocational provision, need to be finally surmounted. Looking at the patterns in family formation, the strong relationship between the young family, the poor family and the unstable family is noticeably connected to unemployment amongst young people. The weaknesses in the education system which have led to a high number of unqualified school-leavers aside, the efforts to affect unemployment amongst young people, the notable example being the New Deal for Young People, have been comparatively unsuccessful.

While the will to move the unemployed into work is there, the government's strategies so far have proved to be ineffective. With jobs available for a high proportion of those currently unemployed, the problem centres on a lack of motivation to leave welfare dependency. This relates in part to the education issues discussed above and their effect on employment prospects, but also to ineffective mechanisms to move claimants off welfare i.e. the existence of 'poverty traps' and the system's in-built option of not working though able.

Tax arrangements

Income-splitting

Informal childcare should be recognised within income tax arrangements for registered parents (regardless of marital status). This would be possible through a tax system which accounted for the dependent status of children as well as non-working and low-earning (for example through part-time employment) partners by pooling the family income, dividing it by a quotient based on family size, and applying the relevant tax formula according to income level. This would help increase recognition of childcare as well as facilitate it, help foster mutual (rather than one-way) dependency and an equal division of labour between parents.

Non-resident parent responsibility

Financial child support
Child maintenance needs to be simplified and made universal by being taken automatically out of wages or social assistance (whatever the income earned or un-earned) through HM Revenue and Customs. In the event of separation non-resident working parents should also continue to receive a dependent tax-break (as outlined above) on their income as long as they are eligible for child maintenance.

Mediation within divorce proceedings
Mediation between divorcing parents should be a central element and statutory requirement of the divorce process. The purpose of mediation would be primarily to work through the practical and financial arrangements between parents regarding childcare post-separation but also to open potential channels for reconciliation.

Childcare

Transferable parental leave
Maternity leave taken post-pregnancy should be made transferable to the father. This would enable the possibility of greater parenting equality between mothers and fathers, expand parents' options and lessen potential employer discrimination against women on the basis that they 'might get pregnant'.

Appendix 1

Technical summary

Sample: 1,560 adults aged 20 – 35 years old

Methodology: Face-to-face in-home CAPI (computer-assisted personal interviewing) interviewing

Fieldwork: May – July 2007

A sample of adults in Great Britain aged between 20 and 35 was interviewed, with data subsequently weighted to the known profile of this population. The survey was carried out via Ipsos MORI's Face-to-Face Omnibus.

About Ipsos MORI

Ipsos MORI is the sum total of two successful research companies, Ipsos UK and MORI, which joined together in October 2005 to create the second largest research company in the UK. With a focus on social research, media and corporate reputation, the company's 950 staff offer a full range of quantitative and qualitative research services, as well as extensive international research capacity thanks to strong links with Ipsos companies around the globe. Working with hundreds of clients in both the private and public sectors, Ipsos MORI embraces both traditional and innovative research methods.

SECOND THOUGHTS ON THE FAMILY

Tables

Marital aspirations, overview

Table 1

Yes (%)	No (%)	Don't have a view (%)
70	18	12

Marital aspirations according to sex

Table 2

Sex	Yes (%)	No (%)	Don't have a view (%)
Female	67	22	11
Male	74	14	13

Marital aspirations according to age group

Table 3

Age	Yes (%)	No (%)	Don't have a view (%)
20-24 yrs	76	12	12
25-29 yrs	69	19	13
30-35 yrs	64	25	11

Marital aspirations according to social grade category

Table 4

Social class	Yes (%)	No (%)	Don't have a view (%)
SC AB (highest)	80	10	10
SC C1	71	15	14
SC C2	71	19	10
SC D	69	20	11
SC E	54	31	15

Marital aspirations according to education level

Table 5

Education level	Yes (%)	No (%)	Don't have a view (%)
Education level 1 (highest)	75	13	12
Education level 2	78	11	11
Education level 3	67	21	12
Education level 4	51	34	16

APPENDIX 1

Marital aspirations according to relationship status

Table 6

Relationship status	Yes (%)	No (%)	Don't have a view (%)
Single	69	18	13
Cohabiting	79	11	10
Separated*	33	52	15

* Separated: widowed, divorced, separated

Marital aspirations according to parenting status

Table 7

Parenting status	Yes (%)	No (%)	Don't have a view (%)
Parent	62	26	12
Non-parent	74	14	12

Main reason for wanting to marry

Table 8

Reason	%
I want to commit to my partner	47
I want to bring up my children within marriage	15
None of these	8
I think that being married makes for more emotional security	6
For religious reasons	5
Because I want to respect traditional values	5
Family expectations	4
I think that being married makes for more financial security	4
It's important to my partner to be married	3
Other	2
Specific practical*	1

* Specific practical reason e.g. for tax/immigration purposes

All reasons for wanting to marry

Table 9

Reason	%
I want to commit to my partner	58
I want to bring up my children within marriage	44
I think that being married makes for more emotional security	21
Because I want to respect traditional values	16
I think that being married makes for more financial security	14
Family expectations	13
For religious reasons	10
It's important to my partner to be married	10
None of these	8
Other	4
Specific practical	2

Main reason for wanting to marry according to sex

Table 10

Main reason	M (%)	F (%)
I want to commit to my partner	45	49
I want to bring up my children within marriage	12	17
None of these	7	9
For religious reasons	6	4
Family expectations	5	4
I think that being married makes for more emotional security	7	5
Because I want to respect traditional values	5	4
I think that being married makes for more financial security	4	4
It's important to my partner to be married	5	2
Other	3	2
Specific practical	1	1

APPENDIX 1

Main reason for wanting to marry according to age group

Table 11

Main reason	20-24 (%)	25-29 (%)	30-35 (%)
I want to commit to my partner	50	46	47
I want to bring up my children within marriage	14	16	14
None of these	8	8	9
For religious reasons	4	4	9
Family expectations	5	4	3
I think that being married makes for more emotional security	6	6	6
Because I want to respect traditional values	4	6	5
I think that being married makes for more financial security	3	5	3
It's important to my partner to be married	3	3	3
Other	2	2	3
Specific practical	*	1	2

* Chosen by too few to be eligible for significance testing

Main reason for wanting to marry according to social class category

Table 12

Reason	SC AB (%)	SC C1 (%)	SC C2 (%)	SC D (%)	SC E (%)
I want to commit to my partner	54	43	53	42	41
I want to bring up my children within marriage	18	17	11	12	11
None of these	4	7	8	11	13
For religious reasons	3	3	5	9	7
Family expectations	2	4	4	7	6
I think that being married makes for more emotional security	5	7	5	5	6
Because I want to respect traditional values	4	6	4	5	4
I think that being married makes for more financial security	2	5	4	2	4
It's important to my partner to be married	2	3	4	3	4
Other	1	3	2	2	4
Specific practical	2	1	-	1	*

APPENDIX 1

Main reason for wanting to marry according to education level

Table 13

Reason	Ed level 1 (%)	Ed level 2 (%)	Ed level 3 (%)	Ed level 4 (%)
I want to commit to my partner	52	47	47	34
I want to bring up my children within marriage	15	16	14	14
None of these	7	6	9	15
For religious reasons	5	2	4	13
Family expectations	4	4	4	5
I think that being married makes for more emotional security	5	8	7	4
Because I want to respect traditional values	4	8	4	4
I think that being married makes for more financial security	2	3	5	4
It's important to my partner to be married	2	2	4	5
Other	2	3	2	3
Specific practical	*	1	1	-

Main reason for wanting to marry according to relationship status

Table 14

Reason	Married (%)	Cohabiting (%)	Single (%)	Separated (%)
I want to commit to my partner	51	56	41	31
I want to bring up my children within marriage	16	15	14	19
None of these	5	7	10	21
For religious reasons	6	1	5	10
Family expectations	3	1	7	6
I think that being married makes for more emotional security	6	4	7	6
Because I want to respect traditional values	6	3	5	2
I think that being married makes for more financial security	3	4	4	-
It's important to my partner to be married	3	4	4	2
Other	1	3	3	4
Specific practical	*	1	1	-

APPENDIX 1

Main reason for wanting to marry according to parenting status

Table 15

Reason	Parent (%)	Non-parent (%)
I want to commit to my partner	46	48
I want to bring up my children within marriage	15	14
None of these	8	8
For religious reasons	6	4
Family expectations	3	5
I think that being married makes for more emotional security	7	5
Because I want to respect traditional values	5	5
I think that being married makes for more financial security	4	3
Specific practical	*	1

Main reasons for wanting to have children within marriage

Table 16

Reason	%
I think that being married is more likely to create a stable environment for children	70
I want a traditional family	12
I think that being married gives children more long-term financial security (including in the event of divorce)	8
I think it is more socially acceptable if children are brought up within marriage	6
None of these	3
Other	1

SECOND THOUGHTS ON THE FAMILY

All reasons for wanting to have children within marriage

Table 17

Reason	%
I think that being married is more likely to create a stable environment for children	79
I want a traditional family	31
I think that being married gives children more long-term financial security (including in the event of divorce)	22
I think it is more socially acceptable if children are brought up within marriage	17
None of these	3
Other	1

All reasons for wanting to have children within marriage according to sex

Table 18

Reason	Male (%)	Female (%)
I think that being married is more likely to create a stable environment for children	80	79
I want a traditional family	30	32
I think that being married gives children more long-term financial security (including in the event of divorce)	23	21
I think it is more socially acceptable if children are brought up within marriage	17	17
None of these	3	3
Other	1	1

APPENDIX 1

Main reason for wanting to have children within marriage according to age group

Table 19

Reason	Age 20-24 (%)	Age 25-29 (%)	Age 30-35 (%)
I think that being married is more likely to create a stable environment for children	79	77	81
I want a traditional family	26	32	34
I think that being married gives children more long-term financial security (including in the event of divorce)	23	23	20
I think it is more socially acceptable if children are brought up within marriage	18	17	17
None of these	3	4	3
Other	1	1	1

Main reason for wanting to have children within marriage according to relationship status

Table 20

Reason	Married (%)	Cohabiting (%)	Single (%)	Separated (%)
I think that being married is more likely to create a stable environment for children	74	61	72	65
I want a traditional family	10	16	12	15
I think that being married gives children more long-term financial security (including in the event of divorce)	6	11	8	-
I think it is more socially acceptable if children are brought up within marriage	7	6	5	14
None of these	3	5	2	-
Other	-	2	1	6

SECOND THOUGHTS ON THE FAMILY

Main reason for wanting to have children within marriage according to parenting status

Table 21

Reason	Parent (%)	Non-parent (%)
I think that being married is more likely to create a stable environment for children	73	67
I want a traditional family	10	14
I think that being married gives children more long-term financial security (including in the event of divorce)	5	10
I think it is more socially acceptable if children are brought up within marriage	8	5
None of these	4	2
Other	*	1

Main reason for wanting to have children within marriage according to education level

Table 22

Reason	Ed level 1 (%)	Ed level 2 (%)	Ed level 3 (%)	Ed level 4 (%)
I think that being married is more likely to create a stable environment for children	68	74	71	55
I want a traditional family	18	11	8	12
I think that being married gives children more long-term financial security (including in the event of divorce)	6	6	9	20
I think it is more socially acceptable if children are brought up within marriage	5	5	7	10
None of these	4	3	3	3
Other	-	*	1	-

APPENDIX 1

Main reason for wanting to have children within marriage according to social class

Table 23

Reason	SC AB (%)	SC C1 (%)	SC C2 (%)	SC CD (%)	SC CE (%)
I think that being married is more likely to create a stable environment for children	75	68	70	68	72
I want a traditional family	7	20	8	7	12
I think that being married gives children more long-term financial security (including in the event of divorce)	10	3	10	13	6
I think it is more socially acceptable if children are brought up within marriage	3	6	8	10	5
None of these	4	3	2	2	4
Other	1	*	2	-	2

Main reason for not yet having married

Table 24

Reason	%
I haven't yet met anyone I want to marry	29
I'm enjoying my current freedom	12
None of these	13
Getting married is not a high priority for me at the moment	9
I can't yet afford the wedding I want	6
I haven't been in my current relationship long enough	6
I am not currently in the financial position I would like to be in when I marry	4
My partner and I are not currently in a suitable financial position	4
I'm waiting for my partner to propose	5
I'm not sure I want to get married	4
Other	3
I'm not sure whether I want to marry my current partner	2
I haven't discussed marriage with my current partner	2
My partner doesn't want to get married	1
I'm waiting until I want to have children	-
Marriage is not currently available to same-sex couples	-

APPENDIX 1

All reasons for not yet having married

Table 25

Reason	%
I haven't yet met anyone I want to marry	31
I'm enjoying my current freedom	19
Getting married is not a high priority for me at the moment	16
None of these	13
I can't yet afford the wedding I want	10
I haven't been in my current relationship long enough	9
I am not currently in the financial position I would like to be in when I marry	7
My partner and I are not currently in a suitable financial position	7
I'm waiting for my partner to propose	7
I'm waiting until I want to have children	1
I haven't discussed marriage with my current partner	4
Other	4
I'm not sure whether I want to marry my current partner	4
My partner doesn't want to get married	1
I'm not sure I want to get married	6
Marriage is not currently available to same-sex couples	1

Main reason for not having married according to sex

Table 26

Reason	Male (%)	Female (%)
I haven't yet met anyone I want to marry	34	28
I'm enjoying my current freedom	22	17
None of these	12	14
Getting married is not a high priority for me at the moment	15	18
I can't yet afford the wedding I want	9	10
I haven't been in my current relationship long enough	11	7
I am not currently in the financial position I would like to be in when I marry	7	7
My partner and I are not currently in a suitable financial position	5	8
I'm waiting for my partner to propose	3	11
I'm not sure I want to get married	7	6
Other	5	5
I'm not sure whether I want to marry my current partner	2	4
I haven't discussed marriage with my current partner	4	3
My partner doesn't want to get married	1	2
I'm waiting until I want to have children	1	1
Marriage is not currently available to same-sex couples	1	*

APPENDIX 1

Main reason for not having married according to age group

Table 27

Reason	Age 20-24 (%)	Age 25-29 (%)	Age 30-35 (%)
I haven't yet met anyone I want to marry	26	26	37
I'm enjoying my current freedom	18	10	5
None of these	12	13	13
Getting married is not a high priority for me at the moment	9	10	7
I can't yet afford the wedding I want	5	9	6
I haven't been in my current relationship long enough	6	7	5
I am not currently in the financial position I would like to be in when I marry	3	6	4
My partner and I are not currently in a suitable financial position	5	2	3
I'm waiting for my partner to propose	6	5	3
I'm not sure I want to get married	3	4	6
Other	2	2	7
I'm not sure whether I want to marry my current partner	1	2	4
I haven't discussed marriage with my current partner	2	1	3
My partner doesn't want to get married	*	1	1
I'm waiting until I want to have children	-	1	-
Marriage is not currently available to same-sex couples	*	*	-

Main reason for not having married according to parenting status

Table 28

Reason	Parent (%)	Non-parent (%)
I haven't yet met anyone I want to marry	22	31
I'm enjoying my current freedom	5	14
None of these	13	13
Getting married is not a high priority for me at the moment	12	8
I can't yet afford the wedding I want	14	4
I haven't been in my current relationship long enough	4	7
I am not currently in the financial position I would like to be in when I marry	6	3
My partner and I are not currently in a suitable financial position	4	3
I'm waiting for my partner to propose	7	4
I'm not sure I want to get married	4	4
Other	2	4
I'm not sure whether I want to marry my current partner	3	2
I haven't discussed marriage with my current partner	3	1
My partner doesn't want to get married	1	1
I'm waiting until I want to have children	*	*
Marriage is not currently available to same-sex couples	-	*

APPENDIX 1

Main reason for not having married according to relationship status

Table 29

Reason	Co-habiting (%)	Single (%)	Separated (%)
I haven't yet met anyone I want to marry	7	38	38
I'm enjoying my current freedom	5	15	2
None of these	15	11	23
Getting married is not a high priority for me at the moment	12	8	7
I can't yet afford the wedding I want	14	3	-
I haven't been in my current relationship long enough	7	6	3
I am not currently in the financial position I would like to be in when I marry	8	2	3
My partner and I are not currently in a suitable financial position	8	1	3
I'm waiting for my partner to propose	6	5	6
I'm not sure I want to get married	4	3	6
Other	5	3	3
I'm not sure whether I want to marry my current partner	3	2	3
I haven't discussed marriage with my current partner	3	1	1
My partner doesn't want to get married	1	1	-
I'm waiting until I want to have children	1	*	4
Marriage is not currently available to same-sex couples	-	*	-

SECOND THOUGHTS ON THE FAMILY

Main reason for not having married according to social class

Table 30

Reason	SC AB (%)	SC C1 (%)	SC C2 (%)	SC D (%)	SC E (%)
I haven't yet met anyone I want to marry	31	28	28	27	31
I'm enjoying my current freedom	17	12	10	6	12
Getting married is not a high priority for me at the moment	7	11	9	9	8
None of these	10	14	11	18	9
I can't yet afford the wedding I want	4	6	8	8	7
I haven't been in my current relationship long enough	8	6	6	5	5
I am not currently in the financial position I would like to be in when I marry	2	4	5	4	6
My partner and I are not currently in a suitable financial position	3	4	3	4	6
I'm waiting for my partner to propose	4	6	4	7	5
I'm waiting until I want to have children	-	*	1	*	-
I haven't discussed marriage with my current partner	2	2	3	-	3
Other	8	2	3	1	3
I'm not sure whether I want to marry my current partner	3	2	2	2	2
My partner doesn't want get married	2	-	*	2	1
I'm not sure I want to get married	-	4	5	6	3
Marriage is not currently available to same-sex couples	-	*	*	-	-

APPENDIX 1

Main reason for not having married according to education level

Table 31

Reason	Ed level 1 (%)	Ed level 2 (%)	Ed level 3 (%)	Ed level 4 (%)
I haven't yet met anyone I want to marry	29	28	27	30
I'm enjoying my current freedom	11	15	11	7
Getting married is not a high priority for me at the moment	6	10	11	9
None of these	14	10	14	13
I can't yet afford the wedding I want	5	5	9	8
I haven't been in my current relationship long enough	9	4	5	9
I am not currently in the financial position I would like to be in when I marry	3	5	5	3
My partner and I are not currently in a suitable financial position	4	4	3	6
I'm waiting for my partner to propose	6	6	4	4
I'm waiting until I want to have children	*	1	*	-
I haven't discussed marriage with my current partner	1	2	2	1
Other	7	3	2	-
I'm not sure whether I want to marry my current partner	3	1	2	1
My partner doesn't want to get married	1	*	-	3
I'm not sure I want to get married	2	6	4	7
Marriage is not currently available to same-sex couples	*	-	*	-

Main reason for not wanting to marry

Table 32

Reason	%
I am happy in my current situation	29
I don't think that marriage changes a relationship	15
None of these	8
My partner and I are committed to each other without getting married	8
I think marriage is outdated	7
Other	5
Fear of divorce	3
I think that marriage is bad for equality between men and women	4
I would rather not enter into a legal and financial commitment	3
I want to avoid the financial responsibilities of divorce	5
Marriage is not currently available to same-sex couples	3
I don't want to spend money on a wedding	2
I don't want to commit to one person	3
My parents were/are unhappily married	2
I think marriage is for people who want to have children	1
Don't know	1
My partner doesn't want to get married	*

APPENDIX 1

All reasons for not wanting to marry

Table 33

Reason	%
I am happy in my current situation	43
I don't think that marriage changes a relationship	27
I think marriage is outdated	17
My partner and I are committed to each other without getting married	16
I want to avoid the financial responsibilities of divorce	10
I don't want to spend money on a wedding	9
Fear of divorce	8
I don't want to commit to one person	9
Other	8
None of these	8
I would rather not enter into a legal and financial commitment	7
My parents were/are unhappily married	7
I think that marriage is bad for equality between men and women	4
Marriage is not currently available to same-sex couples	3
I think marriage is for people who want to have children	4
My partner doesn't want to get married	2
Don't know	1

Response to the statement 'People who want children ought to get married'

Table 34

Strongly agree (%)	Agree (%)	Neither agree nor disagree (%)	Disagree (%)	Strongly disagree (%)	Can't choose (%)
15	25	19	27	12	2

Aggregate of agree/disagree

Table 35

Agree (%)	Disagree (%)
40	39

Aggregate of agree/disagree amongst respondents who would like to marry in order to have children within marriage

Table 36

Agree (%)	Disagree (%)
30	29

Response according to marital aspiration (unmarrieds)

Table 37

	Strongly agree (%)	Agree (%)	Neither agree nor disagree (%)	Disagree (%)	Strongly disagree (%)	Can't choose (%)
Yes	14	27	19	27	12	2
No	5	14	16	36	29	2
Don't have a view	9	15	26	32	14	4

Aggregate agree/disagree according to marital aspiration (unmarrieds)

Table 38

	Agree (%)	Disagree (%)
Yes	41	39
No	19	64
Don't have a view	24	46

APPENDIX 1

Response to the statement 'People who want children ought to get married' according to sex

Table 39

	Agree (%)	Disagree (%)
Male	43	35
Female	37	43

Response to the statement 'People who want children ought to get married' according to age

Table 40

	Agree (%)	Disagree (%)
20-24 yrs	39	39
25-29 yrs	41	38
30-35 yrs	40	39

Response to the statement 'People who want children ought to get married according to social class'

Table 41

	SC AB (%)	SC C1 (%)	SC C2 (%)	SC D (%)	SC E (%)
Agree	42	40	42	42	28
Disagree	37	36	37	41	53

Response to the statement 'People who want children ought to get married' according to education level

Table 42

	Ed level 1 (%)	Ed level 2 (%)	Ed level 3 (%)	Ed level 4 (%)
Agree	44	36	38	40
Disagree	34	41	40	44

SECOND THOUGHTS ON THE FAMILY

Response to the statement 'People who want children ought to get married' according to relationship status

Table 43

	Married (%)	Cohabiting (%)	Single (%)	Separated (%)
Agree	50	27	38	39
Disagree	28	52	41	44

Response to the statement 'People who want children ought to get married' according to parenting status

Table 44

	Parent (%)	Non-parent (%)
Agree	37	42
Disagree	44	36

Response to the question 'Married people are generally happier than unmarried people'

Table 45

Strongly agree (%)	Agree (%)	Neither agree nor disagree (%)	Disagree (%)	Strongly disagree (%)	Can't choose (%)
8	17	28	29	14	4

Aggregate of agree/disagree

Table 46

Agree (%)	Disagree (%)
25	43

APPENDIX 1

Response according to marital aspiration (unmarrieds)

Table 47

	Strongly agree (%)	Agree (%)	Neither agree nor disagree (%)	Disagree (%)	Strongly disagree (%)	Can't choose (%)
Yes	6	14	29	34	14	3
No	1	4	21	42	30	3
Don't have a view	4	11	28	29	20	8

Aggregate agree\disagree according to marital aspiration (unmarrieds)

Table 48

	Agree (%)	Disagree (%)
Yes	20	48
No	4	72
Don't have a view	15	49

Response to the question 'Married people are generally happier than unmarried people' according to sex

Table 49

	Agree (%)	Disagree (%)
Male	29	38
Female	21	48

SECOND THOUGHTS ON THE FAMILY

Response to the question 'Married people are generally happier than unmarried people' according to age

Table 50

	Agree (%)	Disagree (%)
20-24 yrs	18	50
25-29 yrs	27	42
30-35 yrs	28	39

Response to the question 'Married people are generally happier than unmarried people' according to social class

Table 51

	SC AB (%)	SC C1 (%)	SC C2 (%)	SC D (%)	SC E (%)
Agree	27	22	26	30	20
Disagree	40	43	42	42	52

Response to the question 'Married people are generally happier than unmarried people' according to education level

Table 52

	Ed level 1 (%)	Ed level 2 (%)	Ed level 3 (%)	Ed level 4 (%)
Agree	26	23	25	25
Disagree	35	47	45	50

Response to the question 'Married people are generally happier than unmarried people' according to relationship status

Table 53

	Married (%)	Cohabiting (%)	Single (%)	Separated (%)
Agree	42	12	19	15
Disagree	25	59	49	52

APPENDIX 1

Response to the question 'Married people are generally happier than unmarried people' according to parenting status

Table 54

	Parent (%)	Non-parent (%)
Agree	27	23
Disagree	38	48

Appendix 2

Indicators of socio-economic status in the survey

Social class category

Ipsos MORI work with the following social class categories:

A: Upper middle class: higher managerial, administrative and professional

B: Middle class: intermediate management, administrative and professional

C1: Lower middle class: supervisory or clerical and junior managerial, administrative and professional

C2: Skilled working class: skilled manual workers

D: Working class: semi and unskilled manual workers

E: State dependents, casual and lowest grade workers

In the marriage survey social classes A and B have been combined. The highest social class category therefore, is social class category AB and the lowest, E.

Education level

Education levels are categorised according to qualifications. Ipsos MORI use four levels:

- Degree/Masters/PhD
- A-level or equivalent
- GCSE/O-level/CSE/NVQ12
- No formal qualifications

In the write-up, education levels have been categorised, 1-4, with Education level 1 the highest (degree/Masters/PhD).

APPENDIX 2

Social grade according to education level

	Ed level 1 (%)	Ed level 2 (%)	Ed level 3 (%)	Ed level 4 (%)
SC AB	43	17	11	5
SC C1	42	43	26	11
SC C2	8	23	26	19
SC D	4	12	25	37
SC E	2	5	12	27

Relevant demographic patterns

Parenting according to age

	Parent (%)	Non-parent (%)
20-24 yrs	16	39
25-29 yrs	34	33
30-35 yrs	50	28

Parenting status according to sex

	Female (%)	Male (%)
Parent	57	30
Non-parent	43	70

Parenting according to social grade

	Parent (%)	Non-parent (%)
SC AB	17	24
SC C1	28	37
SC C2	21	17
SC D	20	16
SC E	14	6

Parenting according to education level

	Parent (%)	Non-parent (%)
Ed level 1	21	35
Ed level 2	16	19
Ed level 3	43	30
Ed level 4	15	7

Parenting status according to relationship status

	Married (%)	Cohabiting (%)	Single (%)	Separated* (%)
Parent	71	48	18	73
Non-parent	29	52	82	27

* Widowed, separated, divorced.

Relationship status according to social class

	Married (%)	Cohabiting (%)	Single (%)	Separated (%)
SC AB	26	20	19	9
SC C1	33	33	34	26
SC C2	19	23	17	17
SC D	17	17	18	22
SC E	5	7	13	27

Relationship status according to sex

	Female (%)	Male (%)
Married	35	31
Cohabiting	20	19
Single	40	48
Separated	5	2

APPENDIX 2

Social class category according to sex

	Female (%)	Male (%)
SC AB	21	21
SC C1	33	34
SC C2	18	20
SC D	16	18
SC E	12	7

Education level according to sex

	Female (%)	Male (%)
Ed level 1	28	30
Ed level 2	18	17
Ed level 3	37	35
Ed level 4	10	11

Age according to sex

	Female (%)	Male (%)
20-24 yrs	29	29
25-29 yrs	35	32
30-35 yrs	36	39

Education level according to age

	20-24 yrs	25-29 yrs	30-35 yrs
Ed level 1	19	32	35
Ed level 2	22	17	14
Ed level 3	39	35	35
Ed level 4	10	9	12

Notes

Executive Summary

1. Married majority: In 2001 there were over 11.6 million married-couple families in the UK, and approximately 2.2 million cohabiting-couple families. (*Social Trends 38*, Households and Families: Partnerships, Office for National Statistics, 2008, p. 20).

2. Low-income/family structure relationship, further examples of research evidence: '…There is substantial evidence that women from more disadvantaged backgrounds are more likely to become solo and cohabiting mothers (Kiernan, 2002); that solo and cohabiting mothers are amongst the poorest families in Britain (DSS, 1999); and cohabiting families are more likely to have fathers who are unemployed or in less skilled occupations (Ermisch, 2001). Relative impoverishment and fragility are hallmarks of the lives of these unmarried families.' (Kiernan, K. and Pickett, K., 'Marital Status Disparities in Maternal Smoking During Pregnancy, Breastfeeding And Maternal repression', *Social Science and Medicine* 63:pp 335-346, 2006); research in the *Journal of Public Health* studied the profiles of 1,431 mothers who were booked for antenatal care. The researchers found that, 'Compared with the married women, unmarried women overall were, on average, younger, less educated, of lower social class, in poorer economic circumstances, more dependent on state support and less satisfied with their living arrangements.' (MacDonald, L.D., Peacock, J.L. and Anderson, H.R., Department of Public Health Sciences, St George's Hospital Medical School, London, 'Marital status: association with social and economic circumstances, psychological state and outcomes of pregnancy', *Journal of Public Health,* 1992 March, 14(1): pp 26-34).

3. Millennium Cohort Study: 'Single parent' refers to mothers who were not in a co-residential partnerships with the father at the time of the child's birth; 'highest level' is equivalent to NVQ level 4/5, Kiernan, K., 'Non- residential Fatherhood and Child Involvement: Evidence from the Millennium Cohort Study,' Centre for Analysis of Social Exclusion, 2005, p. 4.

4. Longevity of married partnerships with children compared to cohabiting: *'Focus on the Family', Taking the Long View: the ISER Report 2000/2001*, Institute for Social and Economic Research, University of Essex, 2001, p. 7.

5. Rise in number of NEETs: The Prince's Trust with the Centre for Economic Performance at the London School of Economics, *The Cost of Exclusion: Counting the Cost of Youth Disadvantage in the UK*, April 2007.

Introduction

1. Coontz, S., 'How Feminism Saved Marriage,' *The FirstPost*, 22 December 2006.

2. Coontz, S., 'How Feminism Saved Marriage,' *The FirstPost*,

NOTES

   22 December 2006.

3 Labour Party Manifesto 1983;
   (http://www.labour-party.org.uk/manifestos/1983/1983-labour-manifesto.shtml)

4 Ward, K., Sullivan, A. and Bradshaw, J., 'Income Poverty', in Hansen, K. and Joshi, H.(eds), *Millennium Cohort Study, Second Survey: A User's Guide to Initial Findings*, Centre for Longitudinal Studies, Institute of Education, University of London, July 2007, p. 174.

5 Sanders, D. and Reed, J., *Kitchen Sink or Swim: Women in the Eighties, The Choices*, Penguin Books, Middlesex, 1982.

6 Brooks, L., *The Story of Childhood: Growing Up in Modern Britain*, Bloomsbury Publishing, London, 2006

Interviews:

Professor Michael Lamb

1 Department for Work and Pensions, *A New System of Child Maintenance*, December 2006.

Polly Toynbee

1 Allocation Parentale d'Education (Parental Education and Upbringing Allowance). This is a government subsidy paid to parents without means testing. A parent is eligible if they have been working for at least two years and decides to give up work to bring up his or her children. One of the children must be under three years old.

Linda Bellos

1 Allocation Parentale d'Education (Parental Education and Upbringing Allowance). This is a government subsidy paid to parents without means testing. A parent is eligible if they have been working for at least two years and decides to give up work to bring up his or her children. One of the children must be under three years old.

Kate Bell

1 UNICEF Report. *Child Poverty in Perspective: An overview of child well-being in rich countries*, UNICEF, February 2007.

Esther Rantzen

1 ChildLine and the NSPCC merged in 2005.

Kate Green

1 UNICEF Report. *Child Poverty in Perspective: An overview of child well-being in rich countries*, UNICEF, February 2007.

Annette Brooke

1. UNICEF Report. *Child Poverty in Perspective: An overview of child well-being in rich countries*, UNICEF, February 2007.

2. In 1995 the Swedish government introduced parental leave reform whereby one month of parental leave entitlement was made available for the father.

3. Investment would need to jump from the current spending level of [approx] 0.5 per cent of GDP per year to the Scandinavian [approx] average of 2.5 per cent.

Interview Analysis

1. Finch, N., 'Family Policy in the UK', third report for the project: *Welfare Policy and Employment in the Context of Family Change*, University of York, 2008, p. 2.

The Survey: Gauging Attitudes to Marriage Amongst Young People in Britain

1. See Survey Conclusions for examples from British Household Panel Survey data and MORI.

2. Research was carried out between June and July 2007. See Appendix 2 for details.

3. MORI Polls and Surveys: *Family and Marriage Poll*, MORI Corporate Communications, 1999.

4. The Opinion Research Business: *Young People's Lives in Britain Today*, London: The Opinion Research Business, 2000.

5. Institute for Social and Economic Research, Press Release 2007/05, 'Marriage still the ideal for many couples living together,' July 2007.

6. Bernhardt, E., European Observatory, Social Situation, Demography and Family, *Cohabitation or Marriage? Preferred living arrangements in Sweden*, 2004.

7. Greer, G., *The Female Eunuch*, London: Paladin, 1970, p. 38.

8. Jones-DeWeaver, A., *Marriage Promotion and Low-income Communities*, Briefing Paper, Institute for Women's Policy Research, 2002.

9. Edin, K. and Reed, J.M., 'Why Don't They Just Get Married? Barriers to Marriage among the Disadvantaged', *The Future of Children*, Volume 15, Number 2, Fall 2005, pp. 117-137.

10. Economic and Social Research Council, Press release June 2004, 'Same-sex couples and 'unmarried with children': class, culture and economics still play a big part in our personal lives,' from *Seven Ages of Man and Woman: a look at life in Britain in the second Elizabethan era*.

11 Duncan, S. and Phillips, M., 'Changing attitudes to relationships and parenting,' summary of 'New families? Tradition and change in modern relationships,' in *British Social Attitudes: the 24th Report*, NatCen, 2008.

The Survey: Findings in Full

1 See explanation in Indicators of social status in the survey, Appendix 1.

Conclusion

1 ICM Research/*Sunday Telegraph* poll, 'What Britain Makes of Marriage', July 2007: 70 per cent of respondents agreed that 'It is better for parents of children to be married rather than unmarried,' and 73 per cent of respondents thought that 'unhappily' married parents should divorce.

2 Alan Johnson, Relate Institute Inaugural Lecture 'Strong Families, Strong Society', 27 February 2007.

3 Home Office, *Supporting Families: A Consultation Document*, The Stationery Office, 1998.

4 Kiernan, K. and Pickett, K., 'Marital Status Disparities in Maternal Smoking During Pregnancy, Breastfeeding And Maternal Depression', *Social Science and Medicine* 63:335-346, 2006.

5 Ermisch, J. and Francesconi, M., 'Patterns of Household and Family Formation', in Berthoud, R. and Gershuny, J. (eds), *Seven years in the lives of British families: Evidence on the dynamics of social change from the British Household Panel Survey*, The Policy Press, Bristol: 2000 quoted in *Married or Not: Key Facts, Key Trends*, for Advicenow.org.uk in collaboration with One Plus One.

6 Plotnik, R.D., *et al*, *The Impact of Child Support Enforcement Policy on Nonmarital Childbearing*, Evans School of Public Affairs, University of Washington, 2005.

7 Department for Work and Pensions, *A New System of Child Maintenance*, December 2006, p. 17.

8 Wade, A. and Smart, C., Joseph Rowntree Foundation: Findings 772, from: *Facing Family Change: Children's Circumstances, Strategies and Resources*, 2002.

Policy Recommendations

1 The Prince's Trust with the Centre for Economic Performance at the London School of Economics, *The Cost of Exclusion: Counting the Cost of Youth Disadvantage in the UK*, April 2007.